CARP CHALLENGE

Carp
CHALLENGE

John Bailey

The Crowood Press

First published in 1994 by
The Crowood Press Ltd
Ramsbury, Marlborough
Wiltshire SN8 2HR

British Library Cataloguing-in-Publication Data
A catalogue record for this book is available from the British Library.

ISBN 1 85223 789 9

Picture Credits
Line-drawings by Paul Groombridge

Phototypeset by Intype, London
Printed and bound in Great Britain at The Bath Press

CONTENTS

ACKNOWLEDGEMENTS

It has been a great privilege to work with so many excellent carp anglers and to find such a fund of generosity and willingness to help. I have received encouragement and advice from many quarters but I would particularly like to thank the following: Thank you, Bernard Venables for allowing me to use one of your classic articles from thirty years ago. Thanks also to Archie Braddock, Brian Morland and Frank Guttfield for their great contributions from the era when carp fishing was in revolution. Thank you to those great modern carp anglers, Julian Cundiff, Chris Turnbull, Dave Plummer and Tony Miles, Mick Brown, Chris Ball and Kevin Clifford. All these are household names and for good reason: over the years they have simply caught legions of huge fish and I am quite sure they will continue to do so well into the future. I would also like to thank some of the newer, younger names making a first appearance in this book, all of whom I am sure will go on to great things: Ian Jones, Richard Slater, Phil Humm and Matthew Chapman. I would also like to thank Bob Buteux for the loan of precious photographs and Ron Lees who so quickly and willingly responded with a fascinating tale of his own. Thank you also to Johnny Jensen and Peter Smith, two of angling's unsung heroes and the greatest and most generous of friends. I would also like to thank Bill Barber for his frequent, expert observations on fish behaviour. Above all, I must thank Harry Haskell and Simon Roff for their permission to use extracts from the former's articles in *Coarse Fisherman* magazine. These articles, I believe, illustrate some of the most advanced carp thinking for many years and I am proud to include them as summaries to several of the challenges in this book.

I would also like to thank Len Arbery, Bill Whiting, Dave Davies, Matt Hayes, John Watson, Chris Currie and Mick Wood for contributing such excellent pieces when I needed help fast! Really, after a long angling career I can say that it's the friends made and not the carp netted that make the memories so sweet.

THE DEVELOPING CHESS GAME

Teetering as we are on the lip of the twenty-first century, let us just look back over a century of unparalleled carping achievement and put everything we know now into context. This, I believe, is important if the book we are embarking on is to be fully understood. Remember that the carp is not indigenous to the British Isles. Although it is unlikely there were any in the eleventh century, by the end of the fifteenth century Dame Juliana Berners mentions 'a few in England'. These were probably a developing species in the stewponds of religious houses, in all likelihood brought over from the Continent – possibly by the monks after the Norman Conquest.

It was not until 1836 that a 20lb carp was even seen in Great Britain as far as history records. This monster – for so it was at the time – weighed 22lb and was netted, not caught properly, from a pond in Surrey. For a true rod and line twenty-pounder we must wait a further half-century until 1883 when a Mr Holden took the second nineteenth-century monster at 23lb from the Thames. Not until 1911, however, when the Red Spinners Club began to fish Cheshunt reservoir, did carp fishing lift off in a way reminiscent of the modern era. By 1928 the Red Spinners had taken 22 fish of over 10lb, including the famous Andrews fish of 20lb 3oz – a massive wild carp or, at least, a naturally fully scaled fish in 1916.

Mummery was the Cheshunt expert. It was he who began to foster the legend of the wily carp and he stated that the newcomer must expect a hundred hours of fishing before his first carp would bite. Albert Buckley became the next famous carp angler by catching the then record fish of 26lb in July 1930. He too influenced carp lore by landing the fish on very delicate tackle. Buckley was using 250 yards of no. 1 gauge line, the breaking strain of which he guessed would not be more than 3½lb. His bottom tackle was even thinner and the hook was a size ten. In fact, Buckley was after roach and it is hardly surprising that the battle with the fish went on for over an hour. It was these false lessons of Buckley and Mummery that indicated that carp were almost impossible to hook and then it could only be on the lightest gear which would give them every chance of escape. This was the situation before the Second World War.

It was shortly after the war that the Carp Catchers' Club was formed. B.B. was its President, Richard Walker was its Secretary and the membership was made up of Peter Thomas, Maurice Ingham, Jack Smith, Harry Grief, John Norman, Gerry Berth Jones, Bob Richards, Dick Kefford, Fred Taylor and Bernard Venables. Richard Walker explains how the Carp Catchers' Club came about:

In 1946 I had a book given to me, B.B.'s *The Fisherman's Bedside Book*. This was full of stories of exceptional captures that fired our enthusiasm; I suppose natural human vanity was involved when we said 'Why, we've caught fish as big as some of these!'

It must be difficult for the angler of today to realise what communications between anglers were like then. There were angling journals it is true, but I doubt if their total circulation exceeded twenty thousand copies. Their contributors were limited in number and, often, in knowledge and experience, and there was no real system for collecting reports of outstanding catches. Discussion was not very progressive, being confined, as I remember it, to debates about the value of nylon and fierce tirades against the fixed spool reel which was then beginning to achieve wider popularity.

Because of this atmosphere, Peter Thomas and I were much more affected by accounts of big fish in B.B.'s book than would be today's angler, who reads about several such captures every week. This was especially true of the carp for two reasons. One was that at that time the carp record stood at 26lb and only four or five carp over 20lb had been caught in Britain. The other was that Pete and I rather fancied our chances with carp, having caught quite a number of double figure fish up to some 16lb. Since the author of *The Fisherman's Bedside Book* had expressed special interest in carp and clearly set great store by fish of the calibre that we had been catching, I invited him to come and share our sport. This he did in the summer of 1947 and from this joint operation, I believe, grew what we call specimen hunting today.

B.B., Pete and I planned and carried out hunts for big carp. We corresponded. How we corresponded! Later, we were joined by others on similar quests. Maurice Ingham of Louth, Harry Grief of Dagenham, Jerry Berth Jones, John Norman and Jack Smith. While we were fishing the Mapperley (the home of Albert Buckley's biggest fish), someone came up with the idea of forming a club with a regular rotary letter. I said, 'Let's call it the Carp Fishers' Club.' B.B. said, 'We're doing more than fishing for carp, we're catching them! Call it the Carp Catchers' Club!'. We did.

This was the first of many specialist groups formed to combine the ideas and knowledge of several anglers in an attempt to catch big fish. The Carp Catchers' Club revolutionized fishing. Its tackle and approach were both different from the pre-war attempts of Buckley and the Cheshunt Reservoir men. Dick Walker designed rods and hooks and landing nets for the quest. The members used a new strong nylon line and applied logic and experience to

Maurice Ingham's rod pokes out over Redmire in July 1952. No great evidence of high-tech gear as yet!

the process of fishing carp. There was an element of fortune, of course, in the Carp Catchers' Club's rise to fame. The members' inventiveness and their dynamic wish to succeed coincided with their access to a new, exciting water on the Welsh borderlands.

The Carp Catchers' Club and the lake called Redmire combined to smash carp angling records. In October 1951 Bob Richards caught a 31lb 4oz mirror carp. In June 1952 Peter Thomas caught a 28lb 10oz mirror carp. In July 1952 Maurice Ingham caught a 24lb 12oz mirror carp and then, finally, in September 1952 Richard Walker caught a 44lb common carp, which he followed up in June 1954 with a second fish of 31lb 4oz. Carp fishing would never be the same again. By the end of the 1950s carp fishing was recognizable as the sport you and I know today. There are few carp anglers who do not look back to the 1950s with the greatest of nostalgia. There was an openness then and a generosity of spirit that is not always apparent today.

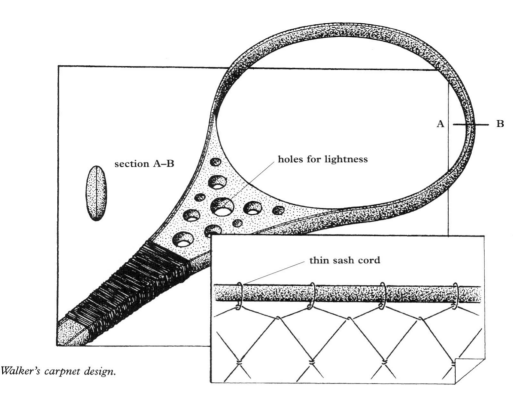

section A–B

A — B

holes for lightness

thin sash cord

Walker's carpnet design.

The carp fishing scene progressed quickly in the 1960s, building on the fabulous foundations that Walker and his friends laid. It was really only then that news of this group of anglers began to leak out. Walker's books and articles were the main source of 'educational' literature, and all of us now entering middle age or over were caught in its slipstream and swept along. In the early 1950s Walker had written: 'It was said of Christopher Columbus that when he sailed, he didn't know where he was going; when he arrived, he didn't know where he was; and when he came home, he didn't know where he'd been. Something similar might be said of the way many men fish.' By the 1960s, largely thanks to Walker, this certainly could not be said of the way that most carp anglers were fishing!

Even my own first carp, caught in 1962 when I was barely into double figures myself, showed the influence of Walker. That fish was not a fluke, I thought its capture out – albeit aided by the great man. The Roman Lakes near Stockport were the place: it was a Sunday, and the water then, as I guess now, was absolutely crowded with people. I wanted a carp, not the roach that the water was packed with, and I knew that I would have to wait until the point of darkness, just before the lake closed when I would be thrown off. I selected a pitch under some alder trees where I figured the water would darken the quickest and, as the daytime anglers began to trickle away, I fed in floating crusts – exactly *à la* Walker. The lake grew still and dark, I knew I had only a short time left before the café shut and the owner began his late night patrol. I can see it now: a black back breaking the silver; a mouth around the crusts; a bubbling; my line slipping through my fingers; a strike, a wild fight and a 5lb common lying in one of those small, feeble triangular landing nets that we all had in those days. I had done it. I had caught a carp by design and not by accident. Even to me, then, I knew that was the important thing. I had done something that Albert Buckley had not.

There were many heroes at that time. Walker's image never faded, of course, but he took to some extent a back seat in the carping world and looked on like some great god as newer, younger faces and names began to emerge. These were all men who had adopted the Walker philosophy and planned their every move in their search for big fish. Nothing was left to chance: no capture, any more, was a fluke.

The name Bob Reynolds inspired us all after his amazing successes at Billing Aquadrome. Bob had baited up a pitch on the water for weeks and weeks before landing some of the largest carp then recorded. His approach, his tackle, everything conformed to the Walker philosophy.

Then there was Jack Hilton who showed some of the most extraordinary dedication ever witnessed, certainly up to that time. In his classic book of 1972, *Quest for Carp*, one chapter describes a 1,200-hour vigil that he put in at a local lake. The statistics are equally amazing: 1,230 hours fished; 8,020 miles travelled to and from the pool; 270 loaves of bread used; 750 freshwater mussels used; 40lb of processed meat used; carp caught, nil! So, despite the work done by Walker and the Carp Catchers' Club, carp were still not easy – and are not to this day. Hilton had to learn his own tortuous way, as we all do! All Walker and his fellows did was make us realize that big fish, big carp especially, could be caught by design and this is a message of this book.

I often walk around top carp lakes and am sometimes a little depressed about what I see there. Many anglers, I feel (and I am not alone in this), are forgetting what Walker and his fellows preached. There is a tendency to think that if enough of a going bait is put in, and if a standard rig with the most modern tackle is used, carp are bound to follow. In many cases, some will: many waters are now heavily stocked and there is enough competition for food to ensure some success for even the most unthinking of anglers. But this really is going backwards: the great anglers do nothing in an unthinking, plodding way. Every little thing they do is planned and considered. Nothing is done without a well thought-out reason. These are the men who make the headlines not once in their lives but over and over again.

I do not believe for a moment that carp are the only, or even the most, intelligent fish that swim in British waters. However, they do show an amazing ability to learn from past experiences and, of course, they are large and beautiful and frequently recognizable as individuals. These individual fish are highly desirable and are often pursued through most of their lives by many men. This, in itself, increases their natural caution and a situation builds up, not unlike a chess game, between man and fish.

It is this side of carp fishing that fascinates me: a skilled, experienced angler pitting his wits against particularly difficult fish in particularly difficult circumstances. Anybody can go down to a purpose-built carp lake stocked to the water line, and catch; it takes a true angling brain of the Walker type to pick out and select specific fish that are very old, very cunning and very large and extract them from the water where everything is in their favour.

It is on these chess games between anglers and their fish that this book concentrates. I have frequently found myself in this position and so have many of my friends and acquaintances – a lot of whom are so generously helping me with this book. I know that you will recognize the sort of problems that we describe to you in the following pages. Sometimes our solutions might be obvious, or feeble, or unsuccessful or even laughable! Perhaps your ideas would be much better. Sometimes, just one of us might make you assess your own approaches. Whatever, the purpose of this book is not so much enjoyment as to try and make carp anglers everywhere think as deeply about their carp fishing as Walker and his friends did in days of old.

1 OLDER CHALLENGES

It makes sense to start with the problem carp of the 1950s and 1960s – really the cradle of our present carp fishing world. This period was, as I have already said, dominated by Walker and his pioneering friends, but there were many others in on the scene and following the action, and hopefully this chapter draws some of them back into the limelight.

Walker, we all have to agree, was an angling genius. Read *Drop Me A Line, Walker's Pitch*, or *Stillwater Angling* and you will see over and over again what makes a great carp angler. Indeed, Walker's thinking is hardly outdated even today, after more than thirty years of progress. Put Walker on the most hard-fished carp water and I guess that he would still catch fish. This chapter is dedicated not only to him but also to the memory of all those who fished with him and helped to create the fishing revolutions, the fruits of which we all now enjoy.

One of the heroes of yesteryear: Bill Quinlan returns a near 20lb fish to Ashlea Pool.

BOB REYNOLDS AT BILLING AQUADROME

In 1958 Bernard Venables published a book called *The Angler's Companion* and in it he described how on 10 August 1957 Bob Reynolds caught three huge carp (certainly huge for that time) at Billing Aquadrome. I first read this account around 1960 or 1961 and was mesmerized by it: you could even say that I conceived the idea for this particular book that long ago. What Bob Reynolds did was the perfect historical carping challenge and at that time really shook the angling world. So let us look at the challenge that Bernard Venables described.

The Water

Billing Aquadrome in the late 1950s was (as it still is) a public pleasure lake. Much boating took place and there was even a miniature railway that trucked passengers around the water's perimeter. The Aquadrome is an old gravel pit with great depth variations, very heavy weed growth and prolific natural food supplies.

The Fish

During the 1950s it was known that Billing contained carp, but only because from time to time big spawn-bound fish washed up dead. There was no record of these big fish being landed at that time on rod and line. However, Bob's ability and keenness were well known in

Bob Reynolds (in the check shirt) giving a talk with his old fishing partner Fred Wagstaff – a pair of fishermen that revolutionized angling thirty years ago.

the area and he was invited to fish the water when and where he liked.

The Problem

It is difficult to know where to begin! The Carp Catchers' Club had only just been formed and many of its methods were only beginning to make an impact. Bob really had to forge the solutions for himself.

Tackle was the first major problem: Bob had to build a rod, rodrest and bite alarm to his own satisfaction. He also had to construct his own landing and keepnet as nothing large enough was commercially available at that time. In the event, he decided on the rim of a bicycle wheel attached to a pole; to the rim itself was laced a sack. The idea was that he would be able to guide any carp that he might catch over the rim of the wheel, lift and detach the sack without having to trouble the carp by touching it or lifting it from the water.

The next problem was the very public nature of the lake. Bob knew that it was highly unlikely that these big, wary carp would feed when the crowds were around, so he elected to fish at night.

Location, too, was a major problem and Bob had to hunt the lake very carefully before settling on his pitch.

The Solution

At one point in the lake, a gravel shelf runs

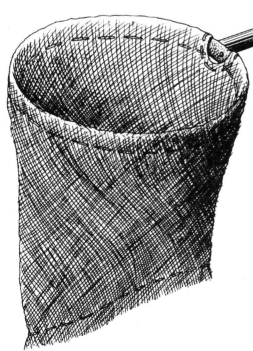

Bob's Billing landing net design, with a cycle wheel frame, sacking for the net and a pole for the handle.

from the middle up towards the bank. Ten yards from the shore it actually breaks surface in a small area four feet by four feet – or at least it did in 1957! Bob rigged up a 'ferry' for himself between the bank and this island by means of a small boat and a system of ropes and pulleys, so that he could ferry himself backwards and forwards.

On the left of this gravel shelf was deep water leading to an island and a mass of tree roots. On the right, the shelf sloped more slowly and had a hard, gravel bottom. It was out along this sloping shelf that Bob began to bait up.

He did exactly what any carp angler would do today and gradually introduced more and more breadflake, then considered to be one of the top carp baits. First of all he scattered the bread in a wide area, but then gradually began to reduce it until he was baiting very tightly in around what he considered to be the prime area.

What Bob did in 1957 might not seem particularly special now, but consider: he had obtained permission to night fish a day-only water; he had built his own tackle specifically for the job; he had rigged up a ferry to move him from the bank to his fishing pitch; he had found probably the best swim in a large water; he had baited up with precision and forethought with hardly any guidelines from the past to help him. Now, *all* he needed to do was land the fish.

This he did on a very stormy August night when the high winds threatened to rip up the island on which he was sitting. In fact, his father who had come to keep him company abandoned him at half past eleven after desperately trying to make Bob change his mind and pack up. It was a good job he didn't succeed! That night, in all the storm and the wind, Bob was to land three historic fish: a common of 24lb 12oz and two mirrors of 27lb 13oz and 28lb 4oz.

Even today a leash of fish like this would make news; then, the angling world reverberated. It is well we remember these old challenges, for without any doubt it was epics like this that inspired people like Hilton and George Sharman, who in turn inspired the Hutchinsons and Yates of today. Hopefully, the exploits of these latter gentlemen will spawn exhilarating challenges well into the twenty-first century.

THE MAPPERLEY MONSTERS

Archie Braddock is perhaps not best known as a carp angler, although anybody who has read his excellent book *Fantastic Feeder Fishing* will know better. In that book, Archie's chapter on Trent carp is unsurpassed; it is probably one of the most gripping and informative pieces on carp fishing ever written and highlights the author's perseverance, knowledge and technical prowess. Of course, all this is to be expected, for Archie has a very long pedigree: he first caught carp way back in the beginning of the

Walker era and has been well known and highly respected for well over thirty years. The problem for Archie's image (not that he cares about that) is probably that he has been so phenomenally successful with other species such as roach, rudd, chub, barbel and pike – to carping fanatics this type of record speaks ill! To some of the carp-only boys any other species is a shame and not an honour – what a lot they miss! Anyway, enough moralizing and on with the challenge.

The Water

Mapperley Reservoir lies just inside the borders of Derbyshire, close to Mapperley village, with the old Shipley Hall grounds on the other bank. The lake's waters were originally used for nearby coal-mines in conjunction with other reservoirs on the road to Heanor, a town on the outskirts of the water. The lake is around thirty acres in extent and at its deepest, near the dam, around thirty feet deep. However, there are extensive shallows, covered with small-padded lilies. The water when Archie was fishing there in the 1960s was fabulously rich with all types of food – including swan mussels, which will become famous later. Sadly, during the later 1970s this once immensely rich water began to decline. The dam broke, the feeder stream became increasingly coloured and the weed died off as contamination from the mining works mounted. As the ecology faltered, so very old, very large fish began to disappear. There are still carp at Mapperley but not nearly the size that once swam its waters. It is a sad tale but at least Archie was on the water when it was in its prime, a prime very well described by Kevin Clifford in his excellent history of carp angling.

The Fish

The fish of Mapperley had been well known for many years and Albert Buckley had caught his one-time record carp of 26lb on 24 July 1930. Strangely, though, Buckley's success was

The Mapperley weed bed.

never really built upon and Clifford's records suggest that for many years only an average of one or two decent carp were taken each season. Mapperley fish, in short, were never easy – but they were huge. By the 1960s Archie Braddock was regularly seeing monsters; these were probably of the same generation of fish that Buckley had contacted in the 1930s but grown on considerably. One huge fish, for example, found dead in the 1970s weighed 35lb even though a significant portion of it had been eaten by rats. Archie is certain that there were several fish in Mapperley at that time to beat the record of the day. He once saw a fish swim through a gap in the weed that he was later able to measure exactly: that fish was between 45–46in (about 1.1m) long, of that he has no doubt whatsoever, and who knows what such a fish would weigh? There were probably, Archie thinks, between fifteen and twenty carp of this calibre in Mapperley when he fished there during the 1960s.

The Problem

Big though the fish were, however, they were never easy. When Archie began his campaign a carp had not been caught on the water during the previous four years. In fact, as far as he is aware, there were only two serious carp anglers at the time and they were shopkeepers who could only fish after lunch on Thursdays (half-day closing) and through Saturday night into Sunday morning. Not only had this pair not landed a fish, but they had not registered a single confirmed carp bite during all those years. We must remember, of course, that these were the early days of the carping revolution and Mapperley was very rich indeed with a relatively small head of fish for the acreage.

At the time Archie Braddock was fishing Mapperley, Jack Hilton was taking carp fishing in totally new directions. Here he is seen with a 28lb 12oz Ashlea fish.

Location, therefore, became a prime consideration. Buckley had caught his fish in very windy conditions when the carp had moved into the area just off the dam. Archie relied on hot, still weather that brought the fish into the shallows and into the weeds where at least they could be seen and approached. Days like this do not always happen in an English summer!

Not surprisingly, Archie concentrated on the carp he could see – in the lilies where a matting of scum and debris built up and where the carp loved to browse, suck and hump the daytime hours away. Now and again, he says, these humps would heave themselves up and would literally leave him shaking for minutes.

Archie came to Mapperley with a tremendous record of success with floating crust and he expected these Derbyshire fish to fall for the same technique. However, they ignored the floating bread entirely. It seemed as though they did not recognize bread as food but saw it as some type of alien substance. They would let crust on to their backs and on to their snouts, but never into their mouths. When Archie tried fishing floating crust overnight he found the same amount of crusts bobbing, sodden and untouched, as the morning light broke. The carp had simply melted away into the deeper water to feed.

Thereafter, Archie dragged holes in the weed and baited traditionally with bread and potatoes. Tench, bream and even roach fell for the tactic, but no carp. Knowing that there were empty swan mussels in the mud, Archie tried crushing these and using portions on the hook. Tench, tench and more tench fell to his rod, but still no carp even though he could see them cruising and browsing in his baited area.

Little by little, during this problem period, Archie began to edge towards a solution. He began to figure that fish were feeding, even if only a little, in the surface film and one day he decided to attack them with lobworms. He used two on the hook, partly to give him casting weight because this was a period long before controller floats. He cast directly to a carp and the worms dropped virtually on to the fish's back. They sank barely an inch into the surface film and Archie could see the tips occasionally wriggling clear of the surface. The carp moved and in the disturbance the worms were lost from sight. Archie kept his eye on the line but it did not tremble, never mind snake away. A few minutes elapsed before he decided to tighten up – the carp was attached. Presumably it had been on for a good five minutes. A flank that Archie can only describe as monstrous lifted up before his startled gaze. Then the fish went down, and down. He cracked off like a pistol. Lobworms did not work for him again.

The Solution

By this time a pattern was emerging and Archie returned to Mapperley with a stepped-up Mk IV carp rod, a big Mitchell reel and 15lb line. The hook was a long-shank, thick wire one, upon which he threaded a whole swan mussel. The scenario was repeated and for a second time Archie found himself connected to a carp that had given no visible bite whatsoever. This time he was ready and walked straight out after the fish into the weed-bed where the water was only three or four feet deep. He followed it at right angles here and right angles there as the carp ploughed around. Finally everything went solid and he realized that the fish was actually showing behind him, between himself and the bank. Archie dropped the rod and picked up the landing net, for it was obvious the fish was now tired and locked in weed. He waded to the fish, dropped the net over it and forced it down until the carp, weed and all, was trapped. In a heaving mass of foam and fish he waded back to the shore.

Upon sorting everything out, he found that he had caught a 16lb 8oz carp, by far the smallest that he had ever seen in Mapperley during those sessions. Archie never had another carp from Mapperley even though he knew there were absolute monsters there. He did, however, tip Alan Otter off about swan mussels and later, after Archie had left the water, Alan went on to catch a twenty-pounder.

A similar thing happened to me some twenty-eight years ago – an event that I have never forgotten. I was fishing that particular summer at Disley Dam, again on the borders of Derbyshire or perhaps just into Cheshire. The water was something like the shallows at Mapperley: very weeded, very warm with carp everywhere tenting, bubbling, slurping and so on. The Disley fish, however, were not particularly large, although large enough at that time for me.

Now, that particular year I landed my best-ever fish in exactly the way that Archie describes. I cast two worms out into the heart of the surface activity and although the line never so much as twitched, there was a carp on the end when I reeled in. For me then it was a big one; if I remember rightly I think it was my first double. That particular method of catching carp – casting natural bait into the thickest of the weed – has appealed to me many times in the past and never have I had line visibly taken off the spool or even along the surface. Probably what is required is a small but visible float very close to the bait which will act as a tell-tale and respond to the minutest of pulls. Still, it all adds to the fascination of stalking, of visible fishing, of the most exciting sort of carp fishing that there is.

A CARP AND A SALMON

I would be wrong to sub-divide this magical tale into the usual categories that this book follows. As a result, you will have to read it and concentrate on it to draw from it the essence of the challenge, which is a beautiful one. But then, of course, everything to do with Bernard Venables' angling life was equally full of grace, passion and humour. I thank him very much for allowing me to use this piece from a collection of stories compiled by John Moore back in 1965. Enjoy it and learn.

I have been thinking of lost fish and fish that, if there is justice for fish, should have been lost.

There was that carp. I should tell of that before I tell you of Leslie Brewer's salmon.

This carp was one that lived in a hidden pool; you could pass almost within yards of it and not know that water lay there. The high dark beeches stood about it, and the thick interlacing of their boughs gave a sense of twilight to the pool in broadest day. There was an eeriness about that pool. Under the trees rhododendrons and bamboo and tripwires of bramble were so blackly dense that you would see not a gleam of water until you had forced your way through. So it was by day; think then of the inky ghostly darkness of that place when night came down.

There in that sleeping-beauty seclusion, the carp lived, it and those other monstrous ones that, if you were very quietly there by day, you

"*France is the only country . . . where that art is brought to perfection.*"

A more peaceful fishing age.

could see slowly cruising just below the soup-green surface of the water. I never saw another soul by that pool; but, sometimes in the rustling, sighing, haunted nights I spent there, I would hear another who came as I did after dark. He would come cat-footed, creeping to his pitch and then becoming still. He would be there and so would I, and we never met or even saw each other.

My pitch was a tiny spit of gravel lying out from the dense press of the undergrowth, and you can imagine what the reaching of it was on dark nights – through the head-high nettle-beds, through the wreckage of that old long-forgotten garden, then down the steep, high fall of bank between the rhododendron roots – and all this with the burden that carp fishers carry. But then at last, in the soft summer dark, there was the water; and, on many a night, there were such suckings at the surface that the setting up of tackle by feel, not sight, was almost impossible for the excitement of the hands.

A cylinder of tin-foil rising up to the butt-ring in the moonlight.

It was as well to have seen the pool by day; the rank, abandoned tangle provided so many hazards that to have any hope of landing a hooked carp demanded that you should know well every detail that lay swathed in the black obscurity. A few yards out from my spit there was a post. It stood head high and rather to the left, and between it and the reaching bushes on the bank there was a channel perhaps a couple of yards wide. A cast need be made well to the right of that post, thus leaving hope that a hooked fish would stay clear of it.

Then there was this night. The bait had been out, perhaps, an hour and a half, and, as on all such nights, my eyes had been fixed to the point of hypnosis on the dim glimmer of the fold of silver foil on the line, and, from time to time, I had shooed away the rats which came slithering over my feet to steal from the bait bag. And now, really, and not as I had imagined it a dozen times, the silver foil stirred, lifted, a shot against the butt-ring, and the line was pouring away.

All went happily at first. The fish was well hooked, it made its long first runs up the length of the pool and, at last, began to tire. Pumping brought it nearer, and soon I was stooping for the net.

It must have been that movement that was the cause. The carp, wallowing and tired, plunged suddenly, and was away again – but not from whence it had come. Between the post and the bank it went now, through the narrow channel and then changing direction, out into the pool so that the line was straining round the post. Thirty or forty yards it went, at a guess, and then exhausted, rolled and wallowed. The line twanged and scraped sickeningly on the post, and there was deadlock.

On my spit, I remembered there were large stones and, feeling with my right hand, I found one. That first shot fell short, but the next fell as I hoped, close to and on the right of the carp. Now, and miraculously, it came slowly across to the left and allowed itself to be pumped back till it passed gently between the post and the bank. Gently it came till it was almost within reach, and then, quite slowly and quite irresistibly, it went into the thicket of the reaching bushes. And now there was deadlock again.

The water there, I knew, was not deep, three feet perhaps, and I edged out into the water till it crept up my gumboots and over the top. My hand found the line in the twig tangle and, again miraculously, the line was free. I started to edge back, towing the carp – from which all fight was now gone. But mud in carp pools, old neglected ones, is deep and tenacious. One foot would not come, and then when it was tugged free, the other stuck. I tugged again, furiously, and suddenly my leg was free, out of the gumboot, into the air, and I was on my back in the water.

But I landed us, the carp and me, and I repeat that if there were justice for fish that would have been a lost one. And so should have been, as I started to tell, Leslie Brewer's salmon last May.

He was fishing opposite me, on the other bank, and I was drinking coffee when I heard him shout, 'It's on'. There he was, on a high narrow bit of bank; on either side of him were bushes and trees, and the water was seven feet below him. He could not stir from that place. The salmon, which was one of the boring, rolling and surface-lashing sort, edged away downstream from him.

Now, as my breath grew short, he eased himself over the edge of the bank, slid down to a tiny patch of gravel under the bank. There was just room for his feet. The salmon, now ten yards downstream, would not run, would not move; it just lay on the support of the line and rolled. Here was deadlock too.

Leslie Brewer tried everything that a man may try to induce that salmon to come upstream, to make it move from that hang on the line downstream. But there it stuck, immovable. Then I threw stones behind its tail, and for a moment we thought it would move up. But soon it began to drop back again, a little farther downstream, and Leslie Brewer could do nothing.

Now the salmon began to edge across the current towards me, and I moved out as far as gumboots would allow in the hope that it would come within reach of my gaff. But soon it was back where it had been. An hour had passed, and thoughts began to rise in my mind of stripping off and swimming across with the gaff. So I might have done, but, at last, the fish began, a very little at a time, to yield to pressure of the rod.

Probably half an hour that took; then it was under Leslie Brewer's feet, and he, pressed back against the vertical bank, got the gaff home. He heaved the salmon over his head, on to the bank above. There it poised for a moment, thrashed and fell over. Now Leslie Brewer threw his rod up on to the bank, scrabbled the fish from the water, and clawed up on to the bank. The salmon was his. For some fish, it appears, there is no justice.

WHEN CARPING WAS FUN

Younger carp anglers might think that it is all too easy to hark back to an imaginary time when all carp fishermen formed a brotherhood and everybody fished in fun and inventive ways. I suppose many modern carp anglers are sick and tired of being labelled the boilie brigade and being criticized for a robotic approach to fishing. The trouble, to some extent, is that many young carp anglers have come into fishing right off this top rung with little or no experience of other 'lesser' species along the way. This was hardly ever the case with carp fishermen who began before the 1970s. Their apprenticeship had been served on rivers, canals and every water type before they moved on to look for carp. This meant that the earlier carp anglers were not totally carp orientated but could think more openly about other species, widely diversified methods and the different ways that fishing can be enjoyed.

A typical and perfect example is Brian Morland. Brian comes from Yorkshire and has been a famous name in the angling press for about twenty years. His fishing has encompassed every type of Yorkshire water – and there cannot be a greater variety anywhere in the world. He made his name with catches of barbel and chub, but he has had many a big roach and tench and, of course, carp. This story begins in 1970.

The Water

Brian knew of a small, private mill-pond. It was very deep, very clear and full of sticklebacks. Apart from that, there was nothing known to live in the water. Now, it happened that in the next valley there was an equally small water stocked with carp and some of these, legitimately, found their way into the mill-pond. Although it was only a small water and the carp might have been seen as naïve, a challenge began to emerge.

The Fish

When the fish were transported they weighed just above double figures, but once in the very rich water they began to pile on weight. It was evident that both mirrors and commons were soon approaching the amazing 20lb mark. Amazing? You have to realize that back in 1970 a 20lb carp would still come close to making the front page on an angling newspaper.

The Problem

So, what was the problem here? In all probability, what made this mill-pond so very difficult was the fact that it was so rich in natural food. Remember, no other fish, apart from small fry, had lived in it before and so the massive food supplies were largely untapped. Carp baits were still very much at a primary level twenty-five years ago and there was little in the way of specials or particles that Brian could introduce to wean the fish off naturals. Therefore, it was to naturals that he turned.

The Solution

The solution in part rested with Brian simply recognizing that the fish were eating natural foods and slotting into this pattern, using worms for most of the campaign. Fish were, however, still very slow in coming. He decided that night fishing would be by far his best bet, but the nature of the banks and the caution of the fish suggested to him that float fishing would have the edge over legering. Remember that in the 1970s virtually all legering meant freelining which was a notoriously inefficient method although we did not know it at the time.

This is where a technological device steps in. Brian had been fortunate enough to have corresponded with Richard Walker over many seasons. Today, he has hundreds of Richard's letters on all sorts of subjects, including fly-tying and salmon fishing. However, the letters around the period in question focus on the first beta-light float. It seems that at this time Richard was working on them furiously. They were pretty primitive, simply porcupine quills with old, brittle, glass beta-lights glued into the top, but their efficiency was undoubted. Of course, if they were dropped and broken the radioactive material spilled out and could be unpleasant.

It seems to have been a fairly hectic, pioneering period. Brian's phone often rang at eleven o'clock or even midnight as Richard had yet another thought about the floats and the carp.

Anyway, the beta-light float did the trick. Very shortly, it went under above a margin-fished worm and a 22lb 8oz common carp was landed. A fish of that size in Yorkshire at that time made immense news and it was not long before Brian was contacted by another giant, Kevin Clifford, and together they began to pioneer carp fishing in the Yorkshire region.

I suppose it is stories like this that can make some of today's approach work seem rather laborious and unthinking. Certainly, the excitement of those early days is hard, sometimes, to rekindle.

THE MONSTERS OF ARLESEY LAKE

We have already mentioned the Carp Catchers' Club, but one man who is not a member possibly had just as much influence on infant specimen hunting – even as much as the most august members of the Club itself. That man is Frank Guttfield. In 1964 he published his book *In Search of Big Fish*, which revolutionized the way aspiring specialist anglers thought and behaved. The book was truly a milestone for everybody learning their fishing through the 1960s and early 1970s and Frank became – and still is – a hero to all specialist anglers.

I think readers would agree that the most gripping entry from the book, which is a record of his fishing years, concerns the monsters of Arlesey Lake.

The Water

Arlesey Lake is a clay pit which was dug around the mid 1930s by the London Brick Company. It is situated on a seam of blue clay and brick-making, along with farming, was a major local industry. In area Arlesey is about fifteen acres and somewhere between fifty-five and sixty-five feet deep. The water came to prominence during the 1950s through the huge catches of enormous perch that Richard Walker and Bob Rutland caught there. The water also contained bream, pike and roach – and something else!

The Problem

As for the problem, I think it is only fair now to let Frank speak for himself:

25 November; Arlesey Lake. The day was very foggy. I had hoped to spend another day after those elusive Arlesey perch but in the dusky conditions it seemed almost a waste of time – I could not see a quarter of the way across the lake. So, instead, I decided to fish for the monsters of the bay. But let me tell you how this story started.

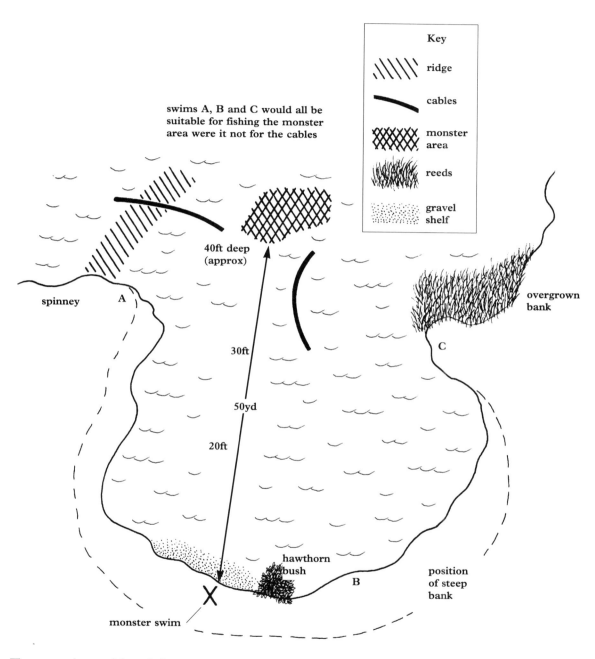

swims A, B and C would all be suitable for fishing the monster area were it not for the cables

Key

- ///// ridge
- —— cables
- XXXXX monster area
- reeds
- gravel shelf

40ft deep (approx)

spinney

A

30ft

50yd

20ft

hawthorn bush

monster swim

X

B

position of steep bank

overgrown bank

C

The monster bay at Arlesey Lake.

It was on a rather summery day in the November of 1958 that Bernard Everitt and I first encountered these rather mysterious fish. We were legering at long range, as we often used to, for the roach, casting about fifty yards into about forty feet of water. These Arlesey roach are no monsters, but they provide us with quite a bit of fun and practice. Our tackles were straightforward enough: Mk IV Avons, 5lb lines, and ½oz of lead. Hooks were size twelve, 4in (10cm) from the lead. Our baits were small bits of crust and flake, groundbaiting was done with the aid of a catapult, and we used tiny dough bobbins as bite indicators.

Just before midday we both started to get the feeblest of flickers on our bobbins, and in fact that was the first time we used the word twitcher. The lake was dead calm, and we knew these were bites and not disturbances from drift and wind. At first we were rather puzzled by these odd line movements; most of them we sat and watched, hoping that they would develop into something more definite. They didn't. Some of them moved the bobbin up an inch, others much less. We thought this was rather strange as we were quite certain that roach were not responsible. There seemed little point in waiting for a run so we decided to try to strike them. Each cast gave a similar bite and after we had struck about twenty times between us, Bernard connected with a fish. You should have seen his face! Round went his rod, well past the test curve, and the battle was on. Bernard had his slipping clutch adjusted as tight as he dared, but the fish just kept going, heading for the centre of the lake. There were no plunges or rushes; it moved slowly and positively. Although Bernard's tackle combination was fairly powerful and would cope with the usual run of fish, I could see that he stood little chance of turning this one.

It was a very one-sided affair. After the fish had travelled about forty yards, there were more than eighty yards of line off the reel, so Bernard decided to get the clutch as tight as possible and really clamp down on the fish in a final effort to turn him. It was clearly a matter

of make or break and, as expected, it was the latter. For a few minutes we sat speechless. There were only three possibilities as far as we could see: carp, tench, or bream. If they were tench they would have broken the record twice over. We also rather doubted they were bream. But carp don't feed when the water temperature is 44°F, do they?

Following that episode, we changed one of our tackles to a carp rod combined with 8lb monofil, still keeping to the lighter Avon gear on the other. The twitches continued on the lighter rigs, but the heavy tackles were completely neglected, even though the baits were identical and only feet away from each other. The next two hours were packed with action; Bernard was certainly quicker on the draw than myself, connecting with five fish to my one. My

Ritchie MacDonald: a modern carp master. How would he have coped with Arlesey all those years ago?

fight was very short-lived, the hook-hold giving way after a few seconds, although I did have the fish on long enough to know that it was no roach! Poor Bernard lost all five of his fish, but not through lack of skill or thought. There seemed to be nothing he could do. With two of them he tried to turn them as soon as they were hooked. Crack! The remaining three he let steam off as far as he dared, just in case they decided to turn around of their own accord. No such luck! They made for the other bank, so that with about six feet of line to go Bernard had to clamp down on them with the same drastic result.

During that winter we spent many hours in the 'monster' bay, but on only one more occasion did we encounter the twitchers. This time we hooked one fish each, or rather pricked them. As with my first fish, the hook-hold gave after a very short time. Bob Rutland arrived just in time to see me hook mine; I had told him of these mystery fish we had lost, so he had come to have a look. While he was asking if they were twitching, my bobbin moved. It couldn't have happened at a worse moment. I was in the middle of a cup of coffee, and so had to make a lightning grab for the rod with one hand. My slipping clutch was adjusted just a little too tight, as after the rod reached an angle of about 45 degrees it was almost wrenched from my hand into the water. Then just as suddenly all went slack as the hook-hold gave.

Since that memorable winter conditions have prevented us from fishing much more for those 'whatever-they-were'. The bay is surrounded by a very steep bank of about nine feet, although when the lake is at summer level (usually a foot or possibly two below that of winter) it is possible to fish from the gravel shelf at the bottom. Unusually, this was also possible in the winter of 1958 as the autumn had been very dry. We did try fishing from the top of the bank on one occasion, but it proved to be quite impracticable. There was, of course, an enormous bow in the line, affected by the least trace of wind, and it also required quite a

Fishing should always be about fun and about proud moments.

hefty dough bobbin indicator to counteract it. A small bobbin would be lifted straight up by the weight of line in the bow, which would make detection of these very feeble bites almost, if not quite, impossible.

It might be thought that the obvious answer was to get the baits into the required spot from one of the other banks, but again there were obstacles – wire cables, in fact. These prevented us from fishing the 'monster' area from either the spinney swim or the 'margin' swim. Perhaps it is not strictly true to say that it could not be fished. What I really mean is that there would be very little chance of pumping these fish back over the cables, although as we did not even get any of the other fish moving towards us

I am not sure I am making suppositions about pumping fish back. However, let us now return to that foggy day in question.

My glass rod was rigged up with a 5lb line, size twelve hook, and all the rest, and was baited with flake. On my built cane carp rod I used a 7lb line and a size six hook baited with lobworm, just in case one of those big perch was still in existence. The flake rod had a ½oz tube leger stopped 3in (8cm) from the hook, the worm rod and ½oz Arlesey Bomb on a link swivel stopped 18in (46cm) away. No ground-bait was used, the monster area being shrouded in the dense fog which also muffled the sound of the tackle as it entered the water.

My first cast produced a typical jerky roach bite, a fish of about half a pound being responsible. After this there was a rather dull pause until between twelve and one o'clock, when things began to get more interesting. In that hour there were three bites on the crust tackle, all identical in nature. Each time the bobbin crept up about six inches – and when I say crept, I mean it. There were no warning knocks or taps with those slower than slow bites. Although very little line was taken, these slow pulls gave me plenty of time to think and strike. I managed to hit them all while they were still on the other end. These were yet another variety of bites that I had not experienced at Arlesey in the winter before.

The next movement came about half an hour later, this time on the worm tackle. Again, it was a very slow pull indeed, though the silver paper did keep going. After about two feet of line had crept slowly out, and the indicator had just about reached the butt-ring, I clouted the fish as hard as I dared. This was certainly no perch! Like the monsters of five years before, the fish moved out in a solid, determined way, heading towards the centre of the lake. Never before had I felt such power in a fish, but, alas, it was only to last for a few fleeting moments. I did not attempt to hustle him, but kept as much pressure on him as I dared. He had only moved out about fifteen yards when it came to an end. All went slack; I had lost my third

monster of the bay, and I was overcome by that horrible sickly feeling.

On retrieving my tackle, I could see that it had not been broken. The hook was still there, and there was something attached to it. As it skipped over the water I thought it looked like a leaf, but as I lifted it clear I could see that it was the scale of a fish – quite a large scale at that! It was about an inch and a half long, obviously the scale of a carp, although what variety I did not know. The weight of the fish will always remain a mystery, although I am convinced that it was well over ten pounds. Now I felt much better than I did only seconds before. Perhaps this was the answer to the monster mystery. If not the answer, it was certainly an important link in the chain of events. What annoyed me was that I did not know whether I had hooked the fish in the mouth and it had come out and caught one of the scales afterwards, or whether I had foulhooked the carp. I can only speculate. However, one thing was certain: there were carp moving, if not feeding, in a water temperature of 42°F. The air temperature was 38°F – not exactly the conditions one associates with carp.

The next morning I posted the scale to Jack Hilton, as he knows much more of these matters than myself. He made comparisons with his scale collection and came to the conclusion that it came from a fully scaled common. It would be interesting to have the scale read by an expert, as we might get an idea of where the fish originated from. It might even have been one of the stock introduced by Hitchin Angling Club more than ten years before. Like most of the fish that inhabit Arlesey, they have confounded us with another mystery. Nearly a thousand carp were put in, yet none have so far been captured. Fifty small carp were also given to another local club who introduced them into another flooded pit, where they have thrived. Not only have they shown a good growth rate, but they have already bred more than once.

Almost in the net.

The Solution

Many of you are probably thinking up your own solutions to the problems of the monsters of Arlesey Lake. A good number of excellent ideas have possibly already emerged, but do remember what things were like over thirty years ago: tackle compared with today was absolutely rudimentary. In fact, it was only the élite few who even had a fixed spool reel. There was nylon line but it was unreliable and very prone to twisting and kinking. Hooks were very often a sad disappointment. There were no

Optonics to make life easy: the Heron indicator, when you could find one, was only really good for steam-away runs not the twitches that Frank describes. Carp bites, too, were limited to bread, worm and potato. Above all, remember that Frank and his friends did not really know what they were fishing for! It was still quite widely believed that carp went into semi-hibernation from September onwards and that a winter carp was a fluke.

Considering all these restrictions, Frank did very well even to know that there was a problem at Arlesey Lake!

2 GRAVEL PITS

Gravel pits have been predominant in the carp scene for about a quarter of a century. The species obviously prefers the bigger, more open and generally cooler water to small, tree-shaded pools where successful spawning, overstocking and a resultant size limitation is also a problem. The great gravel pits of the Home Counties in particular have bred their own heroes, both fish and men. Andy Little, Pete Springate, Ritchie MacDonald, Chris Ball, Zenon Bojko, Kevin Nash, Rod Maylin, Kevin Maddocks and countless others have made tremendous reputations with fish that are almost as well known as they are, like Sally, Heather and the rest.

The achievement of these men on gravel pits is at least as great as that of Walker and his friends on estate lakes in the 1950s and early 1960s. Their contribution has been in the reading of waters, the understanding of the wind movements, the development of baits and end rigs, and pioneering tackle advances to cope with big fish at long range. These are men with constant awareness of the water and the fish and the problems that they present. I remember Ritchie MacDonald telling me of his habitual use of binoculars so that he could comb the water for signs of feeding fish as soon as dawn broke. Then there is Rod Hutchinson, following the wind not just around a single water but even all over Great Britain to find the very best conditions at the very best times. Read any of Tim Paisley's books and this breadth of vision and depth of understanding is apparent from beginning to end.

The problem seeps in when we look at some of the followers of these great anglers. It is common to ridicule the stereotyped bolt-boilie-happy brigade which is prepared to put time and money on a known water with a known bait with a known rig on a known spot – often with known end results! The length of the wait can be the only imponderable. This is not, by the reckoning of many, a challenge.

Of course, not everybody who sits in a bivvy is mindless, but it is true that many are younger anglers who have come into the sport virtually at the top with money and time to devote to their favourite species. I know from experience it is no good asking a young man to begin an apprenticeship at the bottom with gudgeon and dace, not when they see constant successions of glamorous fish adorning the angling magazines. Patience and a slow apprenticeship are not now particularly popular in a very high-tech, high-speed world. There is nothing wrong with this, provided the anglers involved realize that there is more to carp fishing than simple technology. Much gravel pit fishing is done at range and so the fish themselves can seem secondary to the tackle and the bait, and the whole process of angling can become depersonalized as a result.

I would like at this point to tell a barbel story; you might think that it has no relevance but, after all, fish are fish and barbel and carp are not that dissimilar. The river was the Wye and the month was August. For ten days several friends and I sat there with barely a fish. The odd one did come out most days, but the river was uncommonly dead. At night we put forward many reasons for this: the water was too cold or too low, the fish had simply moved around or were not feeding – anything rather than face the fact that we were not fishing particularly intelligently. Indeed, we were doing our best, shovelling in what we thought were the right baits in the right swims and pursu-

Rod Hutchinson holds a huge pit fish; really one of the giant anglers of our generation.

ing the fish with the right tackle. We might just as well have been fishing at long range on a gravel pit with precious little indication at the Optonic!

Most of my friends left, but I continued to fish. The Wye continued to drop and, in drop-

ping, cleared out even further. The weather became fractionally warmer and brighter, with the sun showing for some hours each day. The combination was interesting: for the first time I could actually see to the bottom and what a shock I and a couple of people remaining received! The swims that we had been fishing were paved with barbel and, by the look of it, feeding barbel at that. They were twisting and flashing all day long and yet, try as we might, experiment as much as we could, the barbel still proved very difficult to catch. I remember one early evening sitting in a swim which contained at least thirty fish and I only got one brief knock on the point of darkness. That was it: nothing, not even line bites. In the end, after a great deal of head scratching I stumbled on a partial solution (small deadbaits) and the catch rate rose noticeably. The vital point, however, is that because I was fishing close-in in clear water I could see that my efforts were reaping no real reward whatsoever and I was forced into constant rethinks.

So it is with much long-range gravel pit carping: the angler knows precious little about what

is going on until a line twitches or an alarm sounds. Between these momentous times the temptation is to sleep, read, eat, talk, even play football – or worst of all go to the pub! None of these activities are really the sign of thinking anglers or the solution to working out a carp challenge. I hasten to add that not all gravel pit carping is monotonous and unthinking – of course not – and here are some splendid examples of problem solving on the large scale.

MALLY'S FISH

Julian Cundiff is arguably the hottest new name in carp fishing at present. His dedication, feel for the sport and logicality of approach have brought him sensational catches throughout the British Isles. Moreover, his natural generosity has been of immense help to scores of aspiring carp fishermen. Here, in his own words, is one of his most searching challenges.

I was once asked at a slide show that I was presenting to carp anglers whether I thought it was possible to be selective and just catch the bigger or biggest fish in a water. The question was aimed at fishing a 'super bait' or 'super rig' rather than possibly locating the biggest fish and catching it, so my answer was an unequivocal *no*! No bait or rig on its own will help you to be selective in respect of big carp; you have to go much deeper than that.

It is possible to catch the biggest carp in the water selectively if you can find it, fish to it and stalk it out. You can see your target then and strike when conditions are right. However, on most of the waters I fish where there are a number of fish, the acreage is large and the carp do not use the margins much, this sort of approach is very hit and miss – in fact it proves to be much more miss than hit as some anglers will testify! I approach such a water in a completely different way, in a logical, technical and some would say almost mechanical way. I make sure the fish is present in the water, I put together a bait and hooking arrangement that

Notice the heavy proportions of this gravel pit carp.

A large fish swims through the surface film as the sun sets.

will catch it and many of its brethren, and I fish effectively until I succeed. With a total belief in myself and a determination to succeed, even the law of averages settles on my side. After all, the more I catch, the more likely I am to catch the big one. This is not a new approach or radical method, it is just a way of catching carp that Ritchie MacDonald and Andy Little have drummed into me. If you want it and you are good enough, you will succeed.

The Water and the Fish

I had been following the progress at one of my local waters with quite some interest over the years. Motorway Pond at Newport, Hull, had been purchased by Hull and District Anglers' Association in 1987 and what a purchase it

had turned out to be! Very rich in plant life, a comparatively small head of carp and little pressure from serious carp anglers had pushed fish weights right up and now one or two fish were knocking on that magic thirty-pound door for Yorkshire carp anglers. I had done particularly well in 1989 on Tilery and decided that enough was enough and I would tackle Motorway and its fish the next season or until I caught the carp I had set my sights on. Mally Roberts had first brought a fish to my attention when he caught it at the staggering 29lb 6oz, well up from its original stocking weight of 18lb 9oz in 1987. Clearly, here was a fish with true growth potential and one which could go thirty-plus and a lot more one day. That was my target, now to set about achieving it. I knew it would not be easy but I had the drive, determination and ability to succeed.

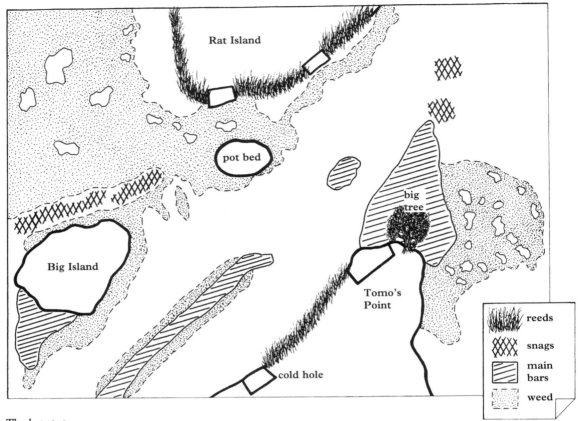

The hot spot.

The Solution

I decided to look at the variables which would make or break my attempt at 'Mally's Fish'. This was the easy part given my experience on other lakes and, give or take one or two things, the same common-sense principles apply: bait; bait application; end tackle; presentation; location; and time – in no particular order.

Bait

The bait problem was a huge head of bream which devoured all boilies with gusto, thus rendering prebaiting a waste of time and making fishing hard work! So I needed a bait that the carp would find attractive and, probably just as importantly, which was fairly bream-proof so

that the carp would have a chance to find it. Initially I did make a mistake on this score because, although I formulated an attractive bait, I failed to make it bream-proof. The mix I chose was:

20oz Big Fish Mix (Nutrabaits)
6 Eggs (size 2)
30ml Nutramino (Nutrabaits)
30ml Salmon Oil (Nutrabaits)
3ml Cranberry (Nutrabaits)
2g Green Lipped Mussel Extract (Nutrabaits)

To make the mix bream-proof I rolled them like donkey chokers (26mm plus). Like mini golf balls, each 6 egg mix made no more than 100 baits, each mix being boiled for two minutes. These were left to dry overnight before I froze them, so making them even harder. I suppose I could have chosen a rock-hard particle, such as tiger nuts, but it has been my experience that such baits are not really selective enough and to get the best from them you need to fish sessions (one to three days) which I was not in a position to do.

Bait Application

Having formulated a bait which I knew the carp would like and made it in a bream-proof way, the next thing was to get carp interested and confident in it. Obviously this would take quite some bait, so I took three weeks off from fishing (which is a long time for me) and religiously rolled six to ten mixes of bait each night. That way I could fish, and fish hard, at the lake each night and not have to miss nights for tedious bait rolling. I decided to bait up for a week in advance with around 1,000 baits every other night and when fishing keep it light whilst my hookbaits were out and put plenty in when I left for work each morning. Hopefully, after a week of bait, the carp would want my food source rather than be curious about it. After all, in theory you have a lot better chance of a pick-up with three hookbaits out with 60 freebies than you have with three in 600. Time would tell.

End Tackle

The water was quite a snaggy and weedy one, so whatever end tackle I decided to use could not let me down. Motorway Pond has a repu-

tation for scores of lost carp so I increased the line strength to make sure that when my chance came I would not be found wanting. The carp were certainly not over pressurized so I picked a basic 'in-line' rig (*see* diagram below) and used 15lb Big Game line straight through. Each and every knot was checked meticulously and from swivel to lead each item of end tackle was chosen for what was most efficient, *not* what looked nicest.

Presentation

As I said, the carp were certainly not overly pressurized and I hoped that I would not have to play around with complex rigs to fool them into taking the hookbait. Inevitably, fancy presentations involve all sorts of Drennan rings, tubing and so on. In gravel pits this may well work, but try it on a weedy, snaggy water and you are just asking for trouble. So I decided on a basic 2in pop-up on a 6–10in Merlin trace length of 15lb rating. To match the hookbaits to the freebies I would need to use large pop-ups. These were rolled round Cotswold ³⁄₄in polyballs and boiled for nearly three minutes and left to dry for two days. No way would the bream make an impression on those. As I intended to fish tight to thick weed, correct hook choice was vital and in the end I went for size one Drennan Boily hooks with a straightened eye. Tests at home pulling against a tree fence always caused the braid to fail first, so I should not have problems with that. Each hook was honed to needle sharpness, and now all I needed was a taker.

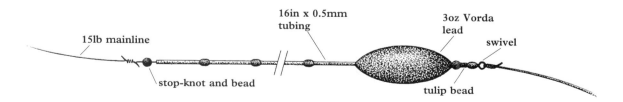

End tackle.

Location

Probably the biggest problem in trying to catch *the* big fish in a lake of about twenty acres is trying to locate it in the first place. Motorway Pond is full of bays, inlets, snags and weed and quite simply the big fish could have been anywhere. However, I would have to do my best and see if I could find it or numbers of carp early on. Actually I was very lucky in that on my very first baiting session I saw a fish which definitely looked like a big twenty- or low thirty-pounder crashing right in the middle of the thickest weed-bed in the lake. Sitting in a parallel swim I spent ten hours one day and saw that fish on no less than six occasions. Particularly as the light started to fall, the carp seemed to jump ever nearer the edge of the weed only to disappear as the light fell completely. The carp had probably laid up in the protective weed in the day only to move out when light levels dropped. Once out of that weed it would be like trying to find a needle in a haystack, so if I was going to catch it, I would have to catch it on its way out of or into the weed. Fishing in the weed was totally impossible, so each evening I baited up around the fringes. I used float, lead and some common sense to find clear areas close to the weed.

As you can see from the plan on p. 32, the area between Big Island and Rat Island created a natural funnel through which the carp left and entered each dusk and dawn. Fishing from Rat Island was impossible, so in the end I chose to fish from Thomo's Point. Here I would have a direct line of pull to the carp and could cover all exits from the weed-bed to the rest of the lake. Bait would be catapulted into the weed and around the edges of it, whilst the three traps would be placed as near to the weed as possible. Provided that big carp did exit from this funnel area as I expected him to, he was as good as mine.

Time

The only times I really expected to have a chance of catching the big carp were dawn and dusk, as he left and entered the big weed-bed.

In effect I had a hot period between ten and eleven o'clock each night and between three and five o'clock each morning. Consequently, I decided to fish each Sunday, Monday, Tuesday, Wednesday and Thursday night, leaving the weekends to recover in. It meant leaving work at six o'clock, getting to the lake after a thirty-mile trip, setting up, finding the clear spots, and hoping. Then, getting up at five o'clock or earlier in the morning, packing my gear up by six o'clock at the latest and getting home in order to go to work that day. A lot of hard work, a lot of miles, no social life and no sleep. Still, if you want something enough, you will do it.

All in all, the planning and bait rolling took much longer than actually catching Mally's Fish. Three weeks into the fishing I had caught twenty carp and at three o'clock on a lovely Wednesday morning my middle rod rattled off once more. Out of the sleeping bag I leapt and, pulling hard into the blackness, I heard a large swirl as a fish was turned over close to the thickest of the weed. Ten minutes later it was all over, and as I watched the needle on my Kevin Nash scales swing round to record a weight of 30lb 12oz I knew I had done it. Three solid weeks of bait making, 17,000 26mm baits, 70 pop-ups, over 1,000 miles in the car and not much sleep, but it had all been worthwhile. I had finally done it: Mally's Fish at its biggest weight and a new lake record as well.

Believe me, if I can do it, you can!

THE CHALLENGE OF BERTHA

The Water

Geens Pit is remarkable: it is only about an acre in extent but has the most interesting properties. The depths fluctuate wildly with areas of shallow and holes that plunge down to invisibility. The weed growth is always prolific and frequently almost impenetrable. In 1984 I counted upwards of twenty different weed types, which gives you an idea of the profusion in this very rich water. For a pit, Geens is attractive and well matured, virtually surrounded by a profusion of trees. For several years the water has been quite intensively fished by a series of syndicate members or those fortunate enough to get day tickets from time to time. All in all, the pressure has been quite high on such a small water.

The Fish

Sometime in the early 1980s, or even earlier, Geens was stocked with some very interesting fish indeed: about twenty or so mirrors and a few commons. There were also two or perhaps three quite large koi carp introduced at about the same time that have always proved impossibly difficult. Of the traditional carp, most were in the teens and I took one of just over 20lb. However, the target fish was undoubtedly Bertha who had been caught sometime in the early 1980s at 26lb and had obviously grown since then. The water also held a few quite large bream (I am talking now about the mid–1980s) and some reasonable tench.

The Problem

Looking back, perhaps the problem was not as great as I felt it to be at the time and, as I have written about it before (in *Carp – The Quest for the Queen*), I will keep things short here. What I did not say in *Carp* was that I felt I was under considerable pressure to be the first to catch Bertha out of the particular syndicate that year. I realize now that this was somewhat childish, but the fact remained that if anyone else from the syndicate had landed her I would have felt that my own particular challenge had been blunted and made to some degree worthless. Whether I am right in thinking this is, of course, a matter of debate and one to which I will return.

However, these were the circumstances: a small, highly respected syndicate, most of whose members wanted to catch Bertha – one very large fish in a small, very heavily weeded pool, with many other carp likely to take the bait before her. It was obviously essential to try to locate Bertha and wean her on to a bait as quickly as possible.

I began by fishing on the surface, a ploy I had

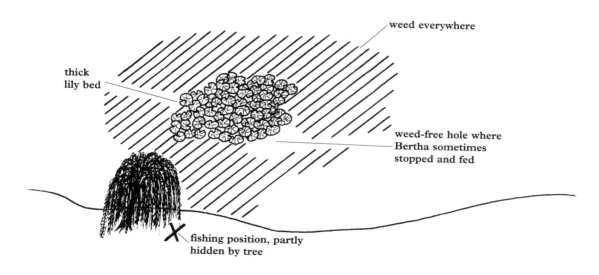

Bertha's downfall.

been told never worked. It did and it didn't: I hooked and lost three fish in the first session. I soon realized that I was unlikely to catch Bertha in this way, especially as she spent her time in the thickest, most tackle-busting of the lily-beds. However, a few sessions simply watching her revealed that she made a few tours of this lily-bed and occasionally proved herself quite vulnerable to a bottom-fished bait, especially as she passed through a clear area. My plan was a simple one: I introduced a very few peanuts over quite a long period into the closest, clearest hole that was only a couple of rod lengths from the bank. Very shortly Bertha showed a distinct liking for these nuts and soon I was able to put a bait in there that she could

not resist. The problem was how to land her: I cannot over-emphasize the weed growth problem. I obviously used tackle that I felt was up to the job and, as soon as I knew she was hooked, piled on unbelievable pressure. I managed to get her head straight out of the water and she was in the net quite before she knew what was happening to her. I am not sure about these tactics for playing a big fish, but she showed no sign of wound around the mouth and I feel in this position the technique was justified.

So, it was a challenge of sorts and certainly one that I was very proud of ten years ago. The challenge to come, however, was far greater.

Bertha is unhooked at a weight of over 34lb.

CHRIS TURNBULL AND BIG B

A couple of years after my encounter with Bertha, Chris Turnbull decided to fish the same water for the same carp. At that particular time he had enjoyed some spectacular tenching successes, and even a trip or two to Redmire and most of the regular Norfolk haunts looked a little jaded to him. He was ready for a challenge and he certainly got it! Chris's own words describe the problems and the solutions of that particular challenge.

The Problem

John Bailey had warned me about the weed and it was this which totally shattered any pre-conceptions I had of the pool being a glorified garden pond. This was no green-fingered orna-mentation, it was an out-of-control mass of vegetation; wild growths of yellow lilies amidst a dense tangle of potomageton and bistort were choked in vast carpets of floating duckweed. Beneath the surface, dense beds of crowfoot and milfoil grew up through the crystal-clear water to merge with the floating mat.

My fishing partner Skid (John Sadd) and I walked slowly round the pool, trying to get a feel for the place. Nothing moved, but, unless the carp were to actually break the surface, the duckweed would ensure that we seldom saw any of the pool's inhabitants. Despite its size, it was obvious that this water was not going to be easy: presentation would be difficult with all the weed hidden under the thick carpet of green, and baits would be in competition with a very high natural food larder. Nevertheless,

Weed can be a crippling problem as well as an advantage.

the pool held a real charm and, of course, it also had promise, for somewhere down there, gently finding her way through the luxurious weed growth, swam Big B.

The next evening found Skid and me back at the pool. It was mid-July and this was to be a short session and really only an excuse to while away a few rod hours; the real purpose of the visit was to put some baits in. The idea was to introduce two different HNV baits and to monitor results on them before deciding which one to carry on with. Mix one was a classical milk-protein bait, slightly sweetened and flavoured with a mixture of maple and molasses. Mix two was based on a mixture of blood, albumin, casein and liver powder. It was a trial mix that I was working on which had proved to be a real winner with big tench, though all the evidence suggested that it took a while to really get them going on it. Just before dark, a small common proved that the same was not true of the milk-protein mix by falling to one of my rods.

From then on, Skid and I took the fishing very seriously. We pooled resources totally by sharing transport and ideas; we also used the same bait. On average, we were spending about three days and nights a week at the water. The fishing proved to be very slow, with perhaps one fish hooked between us every twenty-four hours when they were taking the bait. Their average size was about seven to nine pounds, with a sprinkling of low doubles to add to the records. Bigger fish were occasionally hooked but powered off into the sanctuary of the lilies, never to be seen again. Mix two proved to be a non-starter and was scrapped after two weeks' trial. Mix one they liked; unfortunately, so did the few small tench that were present. We also discovered the carp had a passion for tiger nuts. Rigs were kept simple; pop-ups presented on 18in, 10lb dacron hooklinks, tied off the eye to make a 1in hair; 1½in bombs, 11lb main line, backstops and tight lines. There was never any evidence of the rig not working perfectly, provided you could locate some fish that were remotely interested in baits. The main secret

to success seemed to be remaining as quiet and hidden as was humanly possible. Although these results may not sound too impressive, we were catching consistently and, it would seem, putting well over our fair share of fish on the bank.

The Problem Gets Worse

Each visit to the water found the weed growth thicker and the duckweed denser. By August the whole pool was covered and on a wind-free day would resemble a huge green snooker table. Casting was achieved more by luck than judgement, with only the odd stalks and pads poking up through the carpet of green to guide our aim and place the rig into the odd clear hole in the weed. Each sunk line would cut straight through the duckweed and leave a long dark impression across the surface. On a bad day, two or three bad casts would leave the whole swims scarred with long slits going to each of the bait positions. What a give-away! Still, if the slits in the duckweed could give away the game to the carp, it could also work against them. Most nights the fish would become very active and you would hear them crashing out somewhere in the darkness. In the morning, patches of dark holes in the duckweed would pin-point the areas of activity and occasionally this would lead to a capture.

The mystery of exactly what fish lived in the pool grew and took up hours of bankside conversation. One morning a scaleless fish of 16lb or so was discovered wallowing in a hole in the duckweed; it was an unknown fish. The following week, I held a glistening dark brown fish on a tight line as it thrashed the surface in the middle of the thicket of lilies before opening out a supposedly forged, extra-strong hook. I hate estimating the size of lost fish but she was about 20lb, of that I am sure, and was possibly the 21-pounder that John Bailey told me he had caught. The syndicate record book, however, which had been kept for two seasons, suggested Big B was the only fish weighing over 15lb in the water. That possibility was supported by a netting of the pool during the close-season. Big B had come out along with a number of small fish, but none over big doubles. So the pool was a bit of an enigma – and where were the big commons that I had heard so much about?

By the middle of August the weed growth had become so bad and the duckweed so thick that we were beginning to fear for the health of the fish which had been unable to bask in the sun for weeks. John Geen agreed we should close the lake for a few days and try to get the situation in hand. That weekend found us out in the boat, using a 60ft fine-mesh net to skim the duckweed off the top. The following day a good south-westerly blew down the entire length of the pool. Skid and another syndicate member stood downwind and used 42in landing nets to scoop out even more of the green carpet. Meanwhile, out in the boat, I did my best to dislodge pockets of the weed which had sheltered in the pads, so that the wind could push it down to the nets. By the end of the day large expanses of dark water were open to the sky, and all around the banks great piles of duckweed dried out in the sun. However, a few days later, the wind dropped, leaving the duckweed to settle out and smother the entire pool again.

The Solution

We made our next attempt in the last week in August, when Ray and Pete, two of the other syndicate members, dug a deep ditch from the pool to a stream which flanked its north-eastern bank. Being the end of the pool which faced the predominant winds, the duckweed was gradually blown up and run off into the ditch. Within days the situation was really improving and much of the pool was open.

On 3 September Skid and I returned for a few days' fishing. Skid would have to return to Norwich to work most days but would leave his bivvy in place for me to keep an eye on and return to most nights. For my own part, I decided to cancel real life until further notice. I decided to give the water my best shot and

stay in the belief that Big B was going to fall to my rod any day now.

Up to this point, neither of us had caught a glimpse of the big girl; she had been out in July but we had not been there to witness the occasion. The first night was a total blank, very cold and followed by a clear, sunny morning. I reeled in my baits and topped up my swim with three pints of hemp, a few patches of tigers and thirty boilies, then popped next door for breakfast with Skid who was bivvied up on the lawn beside the iris beds.

While the kettle steamed, I started walking quietly round the pool, towards a newly dug outlet on the opposite bank, intending to poke away the wedge of duckweed which had accumulated and blocked it up. At the far end of the lawn, fifteen yards before the end of the iris beds, something slowly stirred in a wide area of potomageton. I crouched down and put on my polaroids for a better view as, slowly, a huge bulky blue-grey back rose high in the water and glistened in the bright sunlight. The green carpet which had hidden the water for so long was nearly all gone and for the first time I located my quarry. She turned, showing a massive girth, and I suddenly knew that it was only a matter of time before she became my prize. Big B, however, obviously did not share my eagerness; she twitched and wobbled, then turned again before sinking from my prying eyes and drifting under the weed.

I suppose strictly speaking she was right on the far edge of Skid's swim, but after breakfast he would leave for work. We drank the tea and afterwards, before leaving, he helped me move round to the swim in the wood right at the top of the pool. Then he wished me luck and, with a look of deep envy, he sulked off to work. From this swim, the view looked out from between two tall overhanging willows to the far side of the potomageton beds from which I had watched Big B sink from sight. It was just a short, gentle cast away. I quietly set up my bivvy well back from the water's edge and then crept forward to push in the front rodrest.

The sunlight came through at an angle which

allowed it to cut deeply into the water, revealing the bottom of the whole swim with crystal clarity, allowing me to see even the fallen yellow willow leaves winking up from the bottom in five feet of water. Other than a few sparse strands of potomageton, few plants grew here in the shade of the tall willows.

Suddenly, the dark shape of a small double scuttled into the swim from the dense weed-beds twenty yards out; as I watched it, another much longer fish cruised in from behind it at midwater. They chased each other into the middle of the swim; for a moment I thought it was Big B, but realized with a start that it was too long and lacked her depth. Then, with a flick, the fish twisted round in pursuit of the smaller carp and I swear that as it turned I glimpsed its pattern of symmetrical scales. It was a common, a huge common, a mid-twenty at least and possibly a fair bit more. Then, as quickly as they had come, the fish were gone again.

Quietly and accurately, I flicked out two baited rigs into two small channels in the potomageton at the back of the swim. I then took plenty of time to flick thirty boilies closely around my hookbaits. With both Big B and the big common close by, the last thing I wanted to do was to disturb the swim. After perhaps an hour, the trap was set and by this time the sun had moved round so that, even with my polaroids, all I could see in my swim was the surface glare. Over the course of the afternoon, a thin layer of duckweed drifted over the swim and ensured that there would be no more sightings today. Apart from a few trips to unblock the overflow, the rest of the day proved uneventful, but every minute felt like the lull before the storm.

That night the feeling never left me. It intensified as, just before dark, several fish crashed in the weed-bed beyond my bait. Under the willows it became so dark that, apart from the stars twinkling through the branches, the only visible objects were the two bright isotopes hanging heavily half-way down the invisible needles. Sleep was hard won and restless. A little before midnight, a rat scavenging in the entrance of my bivvy woke me from a chilled sleep. I do not care for rats at the best of times but in the pitch black I loathe them, so I threw half a loaf of bread far back into the trees to divert their attentions before slipping back into my sleeping bag. As I lay there, looking up at the huge expanse of stars through the black canopy of trees, I was brought back to earth with a jolt as a high pitched peep in my left-hand Optonic suddenly broke the silence.

Despite my high expectations, the short tussle resulted only in a small common which barely broke into double figures. I sacked it in the deep margins, then set about clearing the mass of downtrodden sleeping bags which lay characteristically between the bivvy and my rods. Just before dawn, the whole exercise was repeated with the capture of a pretty twelve-pound mirror. Such captures from the pool were usually very welcome, but that night they were not; their disturbance may well have put the bigger fish on guard or even scared them out of the area altogether.

By midday the pool seemed dead, the only movement being the constant scatterings of small roach fleeing from the attention of the ever hungry jacks. From my pitch I could see most of the pool and there was no evidence of carp anywhere. The hot sun shimmered heavily on the water and under the willows small flies were becoming troublesome.

Several times that day I had quietly strolled round to unblock the outlet and let out the rest of the duckweed. Now that it was almost all gone, the water really looked pretty, just like a classic carp pool should look. Normally I am loath to leave my rods, but getting rid of the duckweed had become almost as important as catching B! Anyway, the carp in John's pool never feed at midday and the outlet was only thirty yards from my swim, so I wasn't far from the rods.

So there I was, standing with my stick, happily poking away at the collection of sticks, bits of weed and, of course, duckweed, when a single anonymous peep drifted menacingly across from my swim. I looked up expectantly, wondering if it had been perhaps a liner or a bird hitting the line. Ten seconds passed and I decided it was better to play safe than be sorry, so quickly started back towards the rods. 'Peep' came my second call to order then, as a quickening progression of isolated peeps merged into a continuous note, the heavy bobbin hit the top of the needle and the handle of the left-hand reel started to churn slowly.

Needless to say, the few seconds it took me to get back to the rod seemed like an eternity. I knew from that very first peep that B had come knocking. I reached out for the rod, just as the handle stopped spinning; picking it up, I wound down and pulled, and fifteen yards out into the potomageton a hole appeared in the floating leaves. Pulling hard, the 2lb test carbon went well past its fighting curve and, one foot at a time, the 11lb line lifted up out of the weed. For a good twenty seconds all remained solid then, thump, she moved and as she struggled I stepped back, gained a few inches and felt her move again. She was coming now, very slowly and still getting stuck on the way, but nevertheless, she was on the move.

On the scales, she weighed 32lb 8oz which was exactly the same weight as she had been on the last visit to the bank. John Bailey was right, she is a fabulous creature and was well worth all my effort.

THE GRAVEYARD

The Water

The Graveyard was in fact my own name for Booton Pit in mid North Norfolk. The water is an old one, probably dug as a marl or clay pit at least 150 years ago. It is between two and three acres, virtually triangular with a host of irregular depths. It has a varied weed growth for a water that is not particular rich, and is generally murky. Reeds grow on the shallower bars. Partly because it is an old water and dug-over clay, the water is only moderately rich, but

The Graveyard in July.

that has not greatly inhibited the growth of the carp. For a period the bream grew to quite a large size, and there are still numbers of pike of modest proportions. At one time it was a good perch water, and there are still some tench and roach present.

The Fish

Carp were stocked some time in the late 1950s or early 1960s. By the turn of the 1970s it was realised that Booton was a carp water of increasing importance. I first fished it in 1967 and again in 1973 with dear William Whiting who, I remember, one night achieved the miracle of a run on a bait the size of a tangerine! That same year, I lost a fish on a margin-fished crust. It was soon obvious to many carp anglers that there were twenty- and even thirty-pounders in the water – very serious fish then and, I suppose, even now.

The Problem

By the mid 1970s Booton Pit had become a very heavily pressurized water, and there was an increasing number of long-stay anglers. By the late 1970s tight lines had taken over and twanged around the lake like so many cheese-wires. Certainly, by 1980 the carp had become extremely neurotic and were rarely seen unless you spent long hours in the hottest weather, dangling from the overhanging trees. It became obvious that the carp increasingly restricted their movements to a heavily weeded area as near the middle as they could find. There was great jostling for the swims that gave the best lines of attack into this cherished area. At the time, I felt very sorry for the local pleasure anglers who had seen the whole character of their beloved water changed. The banks became increasingly worn down and there tended to be a litter problem. In fact, the water was only kept decent by hard-working gangs of local officials. Naturally, I think many of us also felt sorry for the carp.

Solutions

Carp did, of course, come out of Booton Pit, but every fish was very hard won indeed. Dan Leary won great notoriety for pioneering winter fishing on the water and he had some success for at least a couple of years by fishing intensively towards the back end.

Gerry Morris also set the water alight. His full story is told in *Carp – The Quest for the Queen.* What many readers of that book do not realize is just how extraordinary that first carp of his was. I do not think Gerry will mind me saying that until then he had only caught one other carp; for him to go to one of the hardest carp waters of the country and bag a thirty was nothing short of miraculous. However, perhaps the fact that he arrived at Booton without any preconceived ideas helped him. He took great

Gerry Morris holds one of the largest fish ever recorded from the Graveyard.

care over his bait and even greater care over how he introduced it to the water. He put out one bait every minute – a task that took him hours. The rest is history and his care certainly paid off.

It was in 1987 that I decided to attack the water myself. I spent many days simply investigating, not taking any tackle with me at all. I began to realize that on the very point of dawn there would be certain amounts of movement in various and fancied parts of the lake. I must add that this was very cautious and there were times when I simply suspected the activity of small tench or bream. However, the sight of a very large, rolling common on my fourth visit soon changed my mind.

I began to concentrate on the narrow end of the lake where a reed fringe ran parallel to the bank. On three separate journeys I witnessed these being bent back quite strongly and occasional patches of bubbles rising. My belief grew that the fish moved out of their citadel area sometime during the night to patrol the lake and feed quite heavily. I certainly liked the look of this reed fringe for several reasons and I began to concentrate all my thoughts upon it.

It has to be said that all this activity was completely unwitnessed by the long-stay men. Generally, it appeared that they slept most heavily between one and seven o'clock when the carp, in fact, were at their most active.

I chose casters as a bait as I felt these were as far from boilies as possible. The water had been absolutely saturated with boilies for many years and, no matter what colour, size or flavour, a boilie is surely still a boilie! I only introduced the casters (about two pints each time) at half past three in the morning, or just on the brink of dark and light. I did this to minimize the intrusions of small fish. There was no doubt about it that by half past four on the last two mornings the casters were exciting attention from bubbling fish.

I moved in on the fourth morning. I used float tackle which I cast hard up against the reed-bed. I figured that the fish would not be able to distinguish the line at all well as it lay against the roots. This had to work in my favour as I was convinced all the carp in the lake were very wary of any line in any breaking strain.

I did not have a great deal of time to wait; after about forty-five minutes the float lifted perfectly and slid away. A very large carp boiled on the surface and surged away down towards the deeper part of the lake. Its power caught me totally by surprise and it went straight through a patch of lilies where the hook pulled.

I never tried again. I was satisfied that an alternative approach would work with comparatively little effort but with much greater observation and far more intricate preparation.

The challenge just related dovetails very well with a piece by Harry Haskell on carp and bait and I think it is wise to print it here to show that I am not alone in thinking that there is life after the boilie.

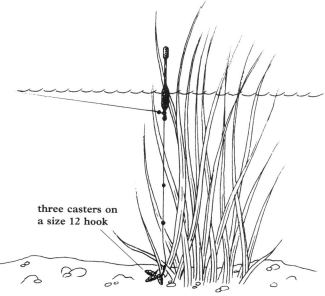

three casters on
a size 12 hook

Float fishing at the Graveyard.

Harry Haskell on Bait
I believe, no, I know, that general carp fishing in Great Britain has for some years become stereotyped in approach, attitude, tactical application and thinking. I can see little meaningful progress since about 1985. I have been asked many times: is there life after the boilie? The answer can only be yes, but how this is to be achieved is unknown to me at the moment. However, there is little doubt that on some waters carp are now being caught in spite of using boilies, the penalty being the 'tame factor'. Then again, was it not always so?

Boilies are such a convenient and successful bait that probably nine out of ten carpers use them. Unfortunately nine out of ten carp on many waters are not easily accepting those with a string attached. It is the past and present success of any bait and its application which hinders innovation on our part. This will, or perhaps already has, entrapped us all.

Although the range of known alternative carp baits is substantial by contrast, the number of alternative tactical applications is very small. Remember that change is constant; we might influence it, but not prevent it. Ironically, change is only discernible retrospectively. So all this may mean it will happen, but as yet I have not seen it.

Many anglers will not recognize or feel that change is even desirable. They are currently trying to evaluate and apply that which has passed. Experienced carpers might identify with what has been said to date. Yet the irony is that it is these established lads who are least likely to be able to contribute to any significant and fundamental change. This is simply because they are, by definition, locked into the traditional thinking mode, hog-tied by their perception, age and experience and, despite all my squirming, I am still with them and I have little doubt that most of you are as well. A change in carpers' perception may well be required to find the key to our shackles.

Change has occurred through 'improved tackle' and so on, which individually may or may not be seen as significant. However, in the overall scheme of things, carp anglers are still doing what they did in the 1970s. Older hands are far too set in their ways and much too close to provoke anything radical. Many of us are standing in the wood, not seeing the trees. We need fresh minds to shift the old order and the sooner the better.

Most in-depth pieces on boiled baits in recent years mention the Wilton theory (with which I hope you are all conversant) and rightly so. If we apply some philosophy, we find that there can never be just one hypothesis, no matter how dominant or reasonable. There must always be at least one other, no matter how unlikely, to provide an alternative structure. Understanding this is important and is why in *Bait Buffs 91* I wrote: 'It is my further submission that Fred's milk proteins unintentionally set us all off on a narrow track. That HNV buffs stayed on this course so long is their fault not Fred's.'

There were and still are two alternatives to the HP/HNV (high protein/high nutritional value) hypothesis, which have proved successful in producing the goods: the opposite, a CB (carbohydrate base), highly laced with flavour, and the middle position, a BDB (balanced diet bait). Despite these alternatives, authoritative notables on carp baits subjected carp anglers to a decade of published material, mostly based on right or wrong interpretation of inexact sciences, together with their own theories as to why using HP/HNV was *the* way to catch more and bigger carp.

At the time, Wilton's thinking was radically new to many and without doubt made a significant contribution to carp fishing, as did those HP/HNV protagonists who later wrote so much. However, their writings became so profuse, persistent and dogmatic that after a decade it became, in some carpers' views, unhealthy.

The alternative CBs (which may have moral implications) and BDBs will, and did, catch just as many and as big fish as the HNVs, and indeed there is no evidence, and never was with hindsight, that HP/HNV type baits are in any way superior in terms of catching on a general scale. They are, or can be, very good baits at times, but that is all and, whilst there is no doubting the morality and value of offering carp a nutritional bait, how carpers were instructed to achieve this is very much open to debate. Certainly some of the science used and the claims made within the written work on HP/HNVs are very unstable to say the least.

It is generally accepted in terms of nutritional excellence for humans that a correct balance of mostly raw, fresh, natural food is unsurpassable. This means unprocessed foods free from the man-made chemicals, colour enhancers, flavourings and preservatives on which so many of us exist. Mother Nature has made it so, and we and all life, including fish, have evolved and survived more or less on this principle. That does not mean that we might not prefer to eat other foods or food substitutes.

Carp anglers have often mentioned just how big their own fish have become since 'the bait' started going in. In many cases weight gain does not mean healthy fish, often quite the reverse, and over the years many fattened-up, old warriors' hearts have pegged out with the stress of capture.

No HNV buff in this world, nor chemist, nor scientist, can produce a boilie that is more nutritious than a carp's natural food. Natural food is or was alive and until we can make life itself, an inert boilie will always be of a lower order. Those who have claimed to the contrary do so from within their own limited perception.

It is more or less understood that a carp's natural food consists of a majority of those creepy crawling things that live in water: snails, mussels, cockles, shrimp, water worms, caddis, bloodworm, numerous types of larva, aquatic flies, nymphs, spawn or eggs, and greens. Baby carp feed on a nutritious soup of plankton, daphnia and so on and will at times, when large enough, feed on fish fry, quite possibly sometimes their own.

There are hundreds of known species of aquatic creatures, but if we just consider the larvae of the midges (*Chironomidae*) there can be several thousand per square metre, in colours red, brown, green and so on. Should your water have upwinged flies (*Ephemeroptera*) or the broad wings (*Caenis*), the nymphs of which can number many thousands per square metre, you would need dozens of gallons of maggot to compete with such profusion, much of which is still alive in the winter.

I wrote about this in 'Rich Pickings', *Carp World 10*, and mentioned the following menu choice available to a carp in rich water. For starters, there is soup of the day or shrimp cocktail or *moules marinière*. To follow, there is a choice of crayfish thermidor with a horn-wort side salad or grilled caddis on a bed of midge larvae. And for dessert, red and green nymphs in spawn sauce or tadpole tart are available.

What are you, the carp angler, offering to compete with this natural food? At best a blend of milk or fish meal powders and eggs, flavoured with Propylene Cylcol 'stinky shrimp', cooked till tough as old boots, with a string attached.

So where are we going, dear friends? More of the same, or perhaps, as many are now doing, seek out new waters with more naïve carp? If only we could rest some of our waters for a few years, we could then begin the sequence again.

All life is a circle, and this is where we will find an answer. For success to be infinite it will be necessary to rethink it again and again. Go back to the start. Workable alternatives to boilies and presentation may well be required.

To end on a positive note, I am pleased to say an innovative form of alternative presentation for hookbaits only is now available. It is known as Bogey and will enable anglers to offer hitherto almost impossible, long-lasting forms of seed hookbaits and so on. This will not be a panacea, but provides options, very interesting ones which are new to the carp.

Bogey

I was fortunate enough to be involved at the start of experimentation with Bogey. It is a clear, colourless, odourless, taste-free sub-

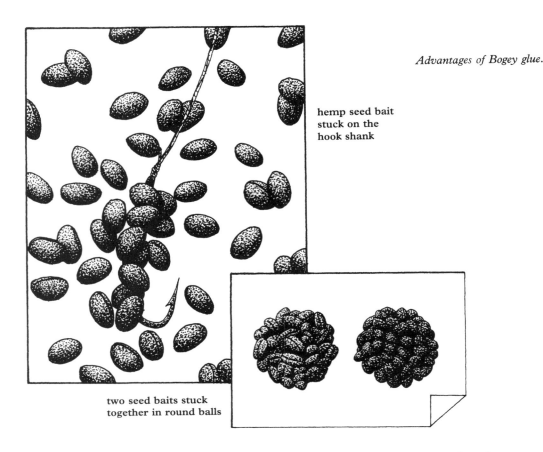

hemp seed bait
stuck on the
hook shank

two seed baits stuck
together in round balls

stance, rather like jelly, which is incredibly useful for making balls of particles that are then easy to hook up. It is safe should a fish swallow it, comes in a plastic tub, but at first can be rather difficult to handle. The secret is to wet your fingers, put them very moist in the pot, grab the Bogey firmly and pull out with a snapping action. Then you rub it into shape. The next step is to apply any dry particle of your choice – any seed or particle that is wet, greasy or oily does not stick to Bogey at all.

Hemp is the obvious seed to use with Bogey but casters are also excellent if kept dry. Live maggots, though, are not very good because they generate a type of ammonia that prevents them from sticking. However, if you scald them first to kill them they will stick to Bogey for ever. Sweetcorn can be rather more of a problem. Loose-feed with tinned or frozen corn and use the dried sweetcorn you can buy from many specialist grocers as hookbait, it quickly swells in water to the normal size. Six grains form a boilie-sized ball or, if you want a smaller bait, glue two grains either side of the hook with a tiny piece of Bogey between.

Bogey is neutral in buoyancy and the weight of the hook gently sinks it to the bottom. However, if you want to create a 'pop-up' particle bait simply smear Bogey around a small polyball and press the seed on to it afterwards. You will find that the whole bait then lifts nicely off the bottom whether mounted on air or sidehooked.

Bogey can be shaped any way you want it: round, square or flat. Moreover, it keeps its shape in the water almost indefinitely.

CARP – OR NOT?

The Water and the Problem

I recently flew to Denmark to fish with my great travelling companion Johnny Jensen. One of the first waters that he took me to visit was a quite beautiful pit of around five acres on the fringes of Copenhagen itself. If you think of a London common pond you could not be further out! Although the centre of the Danish capital is only a few miles away, here the fields are rolling and unspoiled, the pit is in a piece of beautiful woodland and the banks are hardly trodden at all. It was quite remarkable to think that we were so close to such a major European city. The other amazing thing is how very few anglers ever go to the pit, beautiful and mysterious as it is.

What is certain, however, is that the water holds crucians and tench. Some of the crucians are even of a fabulous golden-coloured variety which grow to over four pounds. Fish like this had kept both Johnny and his fishing companion Kenth very busy for a great number of years, but there was always a lurking suspicion in Johnny's mind that something even more dramatic inhabited the pool.

He writes:

On many occasions we had experienced screaming runs on our light match-gear that eventually ended up in broken lines. On other occasions we felt that we had seen glimpses of big carp topping and we became even more curious. The peculiar thing was that even though the water is small and clear and we knew it very well, we never had anything like a conclusive sighting. All this takes quite a bit of explaining and although Kenth and I are both experienced carp anglers, we really do not know why the carp should have been so shy. In fact, the only way, it seemed, to find out if there were actually carp in the water was to try to catch them. No matter how many hours we spent on the bankside watching, we could not come to any proper conclusion.

It always is nice to know that carp have been stocked to a lake.

The Solution

For the first time in my carp career I had to consider a long-term prebaiting programme. I have always had excellent results without having to waste money in this way, but this particular spring I decided it would be worth a try. Something had to be done as we had not been able to contact carp using any other approach. Besides, my freezer was full of boilies from the previous year – boilies I was not sure that I wanted to use as a hookbait anyway. So, looking forward to a week's holiday in May, I started baiting four weeks in advance, two or three times every week.

There were two particularly interesting swims which to me really smelt of carp. One was a reed-bed in the middle of the pit and the other was along a bank strewn with overhanging trees. I became well known and very popular with the coots who soon found a taste for my old boilies. They shot to me as soon as I catapulted the first ones out and began to chew up my well-planned prebaiting programme. They even taught their chicks this trick after a few days. So, I am not too sure how many of the thousands of boilies I put out were actually found by fish!

At last the day came to start fishing and, to my relief, there was no one else fishing the pit and my swims were totally free. I used 20mm boilies so I would not be bothered too much by the crucians and tench – which, for a bit of fun, I would fish for on sweetcorn and match-gear whilst waiting. Remember, I still was not sure if there were any carp in the pit!

Settling back, confident in my gear and bait, I went to sleep knowing that any sound from the Bitechs had to mean a big fish – or so I thought! Several times I was awoken by a screaming indication and seven times I unhooked 2lb crucians.

The following morning I checked the baits and put them out again with stringers on, and after only an hour the line was wrenched from the clip of one of my tree-swim rods. When I struck there was no doubt that this was a big fish and no crucian. The fish succeeded in picking up another of the carp lines and my float-fishing tackle, and it took several minutes and a great deal of panic to clear everything. After that, though, I felt I had fairly good control over the fish, which slowly gave ground and came close to the net – when suddenly the line went slack before I even had a chance to see what I had hooked. I thought the point had slipped but it had broken! Sick with disappointment, I put out another bait, still wondering whether the fish had been a carp or perhaps a really large male tench.

Later in the afternoon, when I was fighting a 3lb crucian on the float gear, I heard a ticking from one of the carp rods. It took me a while to work out what was happening; the sound came from one of the bait-runners and I had forgotten to switch on the audible indicator. I got to the rod, struck and found a fish deep in one of the weed-beds. After a good deal of pulling, sweating and swearing, I finally got the fish through and into open water where the fight was amazingly energetic and short-lived. I looked into the net. I was as happy as I have even been, mostly because I had finally found out about the carp in the lake, but the fact that it was the biggest carp I had ever caught in Denmark didn't really spoil my day either!

WENSUM PIT

What Johnny has just described is a situation that was not unlike carp angling in England in the 1960s when rumour rather than fact was often the only reason to fish certain pits and lakes. Sometimes success followed, often it did not, but even then results could hardly be seen as decisive. For example, on one three-acre lake that I fished for six years, I only saw one carp and that was on the bank, caught by a pleasure angler after tench in 1974. Although that was a lovely 12lb common, I never saw it or any of its possible fellows before or afterwards.

I tend to believe that part of the reason for this type of anonymity on the part of the carp is very low stocking levels. If there are merely a handful of carp in the water there is little need for the fish to move far. Also, the fish may not shoal, and shoaling carp tend to move and be seen. Moreover, if floating baits are not used on the water (and there is no reason why they should be if carp are not suspected to be present) the carp will often not come near the surface for any length of time and sometimes never at all. Should the water be cloudy, the problem of seeing fish is simply compounded. In the early days of English carping, many waters contained only a sprinkling of fish and those were commons which by nature tend to show less often than mirrors. All in all, the picture remains a shady one. Johnny's pit was certainly duplicated in East Anglia to my certain knowledge over and over again during the

1960s and this type of dilemma can still be found.

The Water

Wensum Pit is a very large gravel pit of, I guess, around eighty to ninety acres which was dug in the mid 1970s. The water is largely unfished and, indeed, is generally maintained as a bird sanctuary. It is a particularly beautiful water, sheltered in its valley and already grown round with beautiful trees. In fact, it could be mistaken as a massive and lush estate lake. However, there is obviously a much greater variation in depth with bars and gullies in haphazard profusion. The water is almost invariably gin-clear and throughout the summer and well into autumn exceptionally weedy.

The Fish

The pit certainly contains roach and pike that have made their way in from the nearby river. In fact, it was roach that first drew me to the place with rumours of exceptionally large fish. Early investigations proved that large shoals of roach, some fish well over 2lb, certainly existed and the occasional way they showered into the water indicated that predators were also present. The carp stories originated from mere rumours; legend had it that a nearby estate lake began to dry and to die and was netted for its stock of large mirrors. Only a few were caught but these, supposedly, were introduced to Wensum Pit. No names of the people involved ever surfaced and not even the name of the lake that was netted. No numbers were given of the fish possibly transported and I certainly recorded no sightings in the first few trips – although, however, the summer weather was particularly grim.

The Problem

Most of the problem is already obvious: a very rich, very weedy, very large water which possibly contained no carp whatsoever. However,

A corner of a large pit, well heeled by time and nature.

I rather felt that the water deserved a trial.

Baiting was obviously going to be a major headache. Coincidentally, during the period in question, Julian Cundiff compiled a list of the logicalities of bait application based on:

1. The number of fish known to be in the water. *Not a clue.*
2. The size of fish. *Not a clue.*
3. Whether or not the fish shoal. *Not a clue.*
4. The nuisance fish present. *No clear idea of the number of roach present.*
5. The success of other anglers. *No idea.*
6. What bait worked before? *Probably nothing.*
7. Any over-used methods? *None.*

So, bait was a problem: how much of what type

and where to put it. The one thing I did know was that sweetcorn would probably not be a good idea. I did not want to put in too much time and effort for roach to become a nuisance, much as I love the species.

A Solution

This was September and not a particularly warm one. Bait, therefore, I decided should be sparingly introduced. After all, if there were only half a dozen or so fish they would hardly be likely to settle on to two or three hundred boilies and gobble up the lot. They might go down and pick up one or two, but the chances of a hookbait being accepted would be infinitesimal. So, half a dozen or perhaps ten boilies strategically placed would be my aim. However, to make them attractive, a high odour would be important. I decided on the strawberry-cream flavour and began to make up a few dozen of these strong smelling baits.

The next problem to overcome was where to place the baits. I was highly fortunate in obtaining a very novel type of canoe, a Kiwi made by Perception Kayaks. These canoes are very light (about 35lb (16kg) only 8ft (2.5m) long but a good 2ft (60cm) in the beam. This makes them very easy to transport and put on the water and also very stable indeed. The arrival of my little green craft coincided exactly with the start of the baiting programme and I was able to get out on to the pit and examine the water from above, totally intimately.

Two days of paddling round the pit soon revealed eight or nine areas that I fancied, stretches of gravel where the bottom weed and algae had been cleared. Perhaps the browsers were shoals of roach or waterfowl, but at least these places offered some clues and some hopes. All of them were within sixty yards of the bank so that I could bait and fish comparatively tightly.

Over the next few days, well into late September, I visited the lake every two days, visiting the swims by canoe and seeing if the baits had been taken. Eventually, it appeared that three of the swims showed signs of promise, on each occasion baits had been mopped up. The water depth was about seven feet in each, so at least I knew that the lake's massive swan population was not to blame. Out of those three swims, one in particular had always appealed more than the rest, simply because of its physical beauty on a promontory surrounded by beautiful willows, looking across the valley and down into the distance over fields and woods and spires of village churches. That would do for me.

I am not fortunate enough to be able to devote days and nights to fishing, so I had to plan round several short, sharp sessions; in late September I guessed that the late afternoon till the late evening period would be as fruitful as any. The nights and the mornings were becoming increasingly cold, with even a hint of frost, and the back end of the day would surely see the most carp movement – if any at all.

Now the facts: trips one and two, no sightings whatsoever although on trip two there were a couple of interesting line bites. Trip three, a very large fish leapt out over the baits. Carp or pike? Trip four, no action of any sort. Trip five, a short twitchy run which I hit unsuccessfully. Trip six, a better run with which I connected for two dramatic minutes. There was no doubt that I was firmly attached to a very good fish indeed, something that could not be even the largest tench. However, the weed proved too much, even this late in the year, and the fish was eventually lost. A trip to Scotland could not be put off and the campaign was sadly called to a fruitless end. Fruitless? Well, at least I had proved the existence of carp in the pit and as far as I was concerned the job was more than half done.

3 ESTATE LAKES

Carp fishing in Great Britain began on the stewponds the monks dug for the species that was such an important part of their diet. These stewponds were in themselves probably the forerunners of estate lakes – relatively small, shallow and very rich – and carp obviously flourished in them. Monks and stewponds helped establish the species, but thereafter the spread was rapid. Most of the estate lakes that are now fished date from the mid-eighteenth century, created as part of the sudden increase in the building of stately houses with money from the agricultural and industrial revolutions. Famous designers of the day realized that no hall worth its name was complete without a lake in the grounds, so any stream would be dammed (especially if the land was not productive) to form a lake as a backdrop for a splendid house. Carp were frequently stocked in the eighteenth and nineteenth centuries, but then there seemed to be an upsurge of interest in them from the 1930s onwards. The history of Leney fish is well documented but it was probably only part of quite a wide network of stocking policies. The fact remains, however, that some of the very best carp fishing available today is to be found on estate lakes.

Sadly, there is, or has been, a feeling that estate lake fish are in some way either small or easy. Both these beliefs that grew up in the 1980s are complete nonsense. Firstly, it must be remembered that estate lakes held the British record for at least forty years, and a small water is quite capable of producing mammoth fish provided stocking levels are not too high. That is the key. Ashlea was little more than a puddle and yet veritable monsters lived there for many years very happily indeed. Therefore,

Estate lake morning.

a water does not have to be large at all to produce very big fish.

Secondly, the fact that an estate lake is small, shallow and often clear and the fish can be seen is not always an advantage. The very fact that you are fishing tight and close generally works against you. Carp are very alert creatures, and if an angler does not realize this he is almost certain to miss out on many opportunities.

Where better to catch a carp?

Also, very importantly, estate lakes are generally some of the richest environments that carp can find to live in. This being the case, why on earth should a carp ever open its mouth to eat a bait that is alien to it? There are many times when people have torn hair from their scalp at the sight of big fish feeding hard on any food but the bait they have introduced.

A big estate lake fish is usually a tremendous achievement, and there are estate lakes where fish can go for years without being caught or hooked. These are waters that demand the utmost from an angler; he has to consider every part of his approach, including his physical presence at the water, something that can often be almost ignored on great gravel pits where bivvies are commonplace. Tackle, bait and presentation are all critical on waters where the fish can see the barb on a hook at five yards

and where the splash of a float can force a carp to vacate the area for an hour or more.

Of all water-forms, estate lakes are in the most trouble. Many, as I have said, were dug two hundred years or more ago and are obviously ageing. The silt of generations has reduced many to puddles and many landowners cannot now find the money to put into mud pumping. As a result, every year sees more estate lakes pass into history. Also, as society develops and the need for water increases, more boreholes are sunk and the water table is lowered. This in turn has proved disastrous to many waters and abstraction has halved the surface area of lakes in every county in England. It is frightening how quickly an estate lake can disappear; I have known apparently healthy water dwindle to nothing in just over eighteen months, or two summers. If there is not sufficient winter rain and snow to replenish the water table, the next summer can see a suffering estate lake disappear off the map altogether. That, I suppose, is the ultimate challenge and makes the simple catching of a carp pale into insignificance.

THE BOATHOUSE LAKE

Between 1987 and 1989 I fished the Boathouse Lake with an absolute passion. It was, and still is, quite the most wonderful carp water I have ever visited. The setting is one of extreme beauty and serenity and I do not think there will be anywhere else in my fishing life to compete with it. During my time there I landed about fifteen different fish that were virtually all over twenty pounds. One fish, looking back, was really quite easy, but all the others I found difficult and had to put a great deal of time and effort into catching.

Today, to some degree at least, the secret of the Boathouse Lake is out. In large part this was my fault for advertising its presence in a couple of books and I cannot wonder at the effect this had. Also, of course, other people began to talk as well, but the result is that the carp are even harder to catch. This discussion about the various problems I encountered at the Boathouse Lake and the solutions that I stumbled upon is, therefore, not just for the people who fish from time to time at the Boathouse Lake, but more for the many who will find similar waters and perhaps benefit from my own experience.

Looking out from the Boathouse.

The Water

The Boathouse Lake is a five-acre estate water dug at least a hundred years ago and nestles in a river valley. It is surrounded for sixty per cent of its circumference by trees. The water tends to be very clear indeed and fabulously rich, especially with *Daphnia*. Depths vary from the extreme shallows to areas of four to six feet towards the boathouse end. The boathouse is one of the most remarkable features of the lake: a large, at first sight ungainly, neo-Gothic construction that looms on tall legs and looks out over the entire water. Soon, however, you feel that it is a building of great serenity and beauty and your heart goes out to it. The water lies roughly north-west to south-east and, unfortunately, can catch some very chilly winds from the north. There are also two islands in the lake that add to the general wooded and overgrown look of the water.

The Fish

As far as I can tell, the carp were stocked some time after the Second World War. All the big fish now are leathers or mirrors, but for a while there was a stock of wild fish that grew to about 7lb or 8lb. The vast majority of these seem to have died out. The big, old fish now seem to average about 23lb to 25lb but do not appear to have spawned. For this reason the stock in the lake seems gradually to be dwindling towards an inevitable zero. However, it seems foolhardy to restock with young carp that could bring some sort of disease into a water that many feel is very precious.

The same sort of decline can be witnessed with the other species. At one point there were many roach and bream in the lake but the roach disappeared entirely sometime in the 1980s. The bream became quite famous and certainly a shoal of about a dozen fish contained specimens up to 10lb or 11lb. A few were caught too, I believe, at about 9lb. This shoal also seems to have disappeared. For a short time in 1987 shoals of small perch appeared in the lake but they seem to have perished, perhaps because there were no small fish for them to feed upon. Eels are very rare but, apparently, they can be enormous. The well-known and respected Norfolk angler, Charlie Clay, recently told me of a vast eel that he once witnessed from the veranda of the boathouse that he guessed to be at least double figures. I rather doubt whether such an eel still exists now that there are very few, if any, small fish for it to feed upon.

Problem and Solutions

Carp Awareness of Humans
I soon became aware that the carp were almost

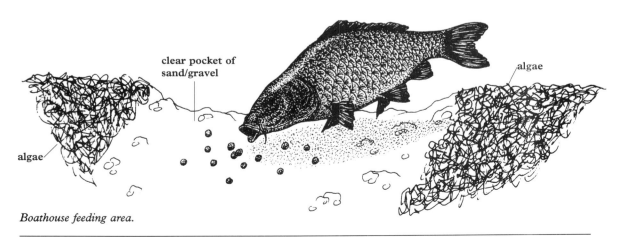

Boathouse feeding area.

instantly alerted to my arrival at the water. Several carp could often be seen on the surface for the first quarter of an hour or so, but gradually they would disappear and the lake would become as still as the grave. I realize now that on very secluded lakes the carp become particularly shy of any human presence and I feel convinced that they can pick up the vibration of a footfall or can even see the angler. This certainly induces suspicion and leads them to the deeper, more remote parts of the lake where they will remain for many hours. I have no doubt that this happens on many remote waters as I have witnessed it repeatedly.

This problem is made worse today as those few lucky anglers who are allowed to fish are usually restricted to the open bank which is quite steep and affords little or no cover, so they are generally totally visible all the time.

In my day, I was allowed access to all the lake which meant that I could get into position as quickly and quietly as possible and then just remain there until the carp became active again and I could spring an ambush. I realize that I was particularly fortunate, but even today there are points along the open bank where cover can be found and an angler can slip in with some foliage around him. This, however, is assuming that he does not bring every piece of tackle with him including the kitchen sink! The Boathouse Lake, and many others like it, demand a slimmed-down approach. The angler has to get in there as quickly and quietly as possible and remain as near hidden as he can.

Weed Growth

The problem of weed at the Boathouse Lake is not a particularly unusual one. There is none of the traditional mid-water and surface weed. Instead, the bottom is coated with a thick carpet of glutinous dark green algae that tends to stick to all the terminal tackle like a draping flag. This, obviously, makes bait presentation very frustrating indeed and you can never be quite sure if all your gear is just lying in a putrefying layer of slime. This does no good for confidence whatsoever.

However, I discovered early on in my stay at the Boathouse Lake that there were areas of the bottom that were quite clear of the algae and that consisted of fine gravel and sand. There is no doubt in my mind that it is on these areas that the carp do most of their bottom feeding. To some degree, these areas are kept clear by springs pushing up into the lake. In other places, the algae is cleared by underwater currents set up by the wind. These seem to be quite strategic points where, for example, cross-currents meet and form some turbulence in the water. Obviously, the carp also play a part. Wherever the sand shows through, the carp will feed and continue to feed, thereby keeping the algae growth at bay.

I am convinced that the key to the Boathouse Lake and many others like it is to locate these gravel areas and put loosefeed and baits on to them. This is not as easy as it may seem: many patches are only of table-top size and accuracy is essential. It can also be a problem finding them in the first place. Swimming is a last resort and it is far better to use a boat or look from a tree (or in this case a boathouse) with polaroids when the light is kind.

It is worth, in my opinion, taking a great deal of trouble over the location of these areas. Just to cast a bait blind into the lake, knowing that it will fall somewhere into the weed is really to waste hours of fishing time.

Bait

A great deal of observation at the Boathouse Lake led me to the inevitable conclusion that the carp there feed naturally on very small foodstuffs. Anything large they habitually treated with suspicion. As far as I am concerned, the answer to this is obvious. Boilies on a rich, little-fished water like this must take second place to particles. Most of my fish fell to sweetcorn but then maggots and casters and nuts and seeds began to take over and fish continued to be caught.

I know that I am a traditionalist and do not use boilies as a natural first line of attack. However, on several occasions I did bait heavily with boiled baits of various kinds and I can honestly say that I only caught one fish, albeit a big one, on these. If I had gone to the extreme and piled in thousands of baits the story might have been different, but why bother to go to this type of expense and trouble when particles work so immediately?

I ought also, in passing, to mention worms. These remain excellent carp baits, especially after heavy rain. This sounds like some old wives' tale, but there is no doubt that a storm does flush earthworms into a lake like the Boathouse and the carp do learn to pick them up.

Carp and Their Fear of the Line

The Boathouse Lake is generally very shallow and very clear and there is no doubt in my mind that the fish quickly learned to recognize lines, tight lines in particular, and associate them with danger. Over and over again I would see carp swimming quite naturally and happily until they came within three yards of a line. They would then generally remain quite still in the water before either turning away from the lines out into the middle of the lake or bolting in obvious panic.

A partial answer to this was to fish with very slack lines so that as much of the line as possible lay relatively hidden on the bottom. This solution did not, however, work all the time and more dramatic answers were often required.

One of my particular successes – and one of which I am very proud – involved trailing a line out to the island, feeding it by hand around the island fringe and then simply poking a bait a couple of yards into open water on the far side of the island. This last couple of yards was of braid rather than nylon. The whole thing took a great deal of effort and I was helped by the very low water of a hot summer which allowed me to put on thigh-boots and literally tread the line into the mud and silt around the island. This way the carp that used the island came across no line in mid-water or even lying on the bottom and the bait was taken very quickly after the water had recovered from the shock of my wading.

I am not saying, of course, that such an extreme tactic is possible on all waters at all times but it does show how important hiding the line as completely as possible can be.

The Weather

The Boathouse Lake is a shallow water exposed to cold winds and the temperature can therefore fluctuate dramatically. I would frequently find that a period of warm weather would be followed by cold north or north-easterly winds which brought the temperature of the water plummeting down. When this happened, carp activity on the surface appeared to cease and the carp totally deserted the shallower end of the lake. In fact, for hour upon hour, the lake would show no sign of activity whatsoever. However, I also found that there would be inevitably at least one feeding spell during the day, often only of thirty or forty-five minutes or so, but provided the baits were in position and looked attractive there was always a chance. This feeding spell was often in the early or mid-afternoon, a period that many carp anglers regard as a low point. My own experiences seemed to indicate that the trough period was between eleven o'clock at night and five in the morning, when I cannot remember anything happening to me whatsoever.

Surface Baits

You would have thought that a shallow water like the Boathouse would respond well to surface baits, but I have personally found this not to be the case despite spending a great deal of time and effort trying to get them to the top. My book *In Wild Waters* included correspondence with Tim Paisley over this point. He remarked that rich waters like Redmire and the Boathouse Lake have a very poor record for floater-fishing and most attempts have come to grief in the past. I have no solution to this problem: my repeated attempts to get carp to feed on the surface have nearly always failed. My only glimpses of success have, surprisingly, been when I have used very large pieces of floating crust. All the modern cat and dog

In at the Boathouse.

The fish is under control.

foods have been completely ignored, but a piece of crust two or three inches square has, very occasionally, attracted the attention of an isolated fish. It may have simply been the size of this floating bait which made it successful, but I would never pretend that I have found a true solution.

Estimation of Fish in the Water

Initially, I felt there were two large thirty-pounders at the Boathouse Lake and one fish that approached 40lb. However, I caught one of the fish that I felt was certainly near the mid-thirties and it weighed about five pounds less, the same weight, in fact, at which Steve Harper recorded it. I feel the mistake that I had made was that I had generally seen these fish at long range and their size, for some reason, seemed to be magnified. Since then, I am very wary of putting a weight on a fish that is more than five or ten yards away from me. Remember that looking through binoculars only increases this problem and an eighteen-pounder can easily look every inch a thirty! Equally, though, when the carp is very close to you in clear water it is easy to underestimate the size of it. Obviously, light and water can play very strange tricks indeed, and tend to exaggerate our natural desire to sniff out new, undiscovered monsters!

Triggers

The Boathouse Lake carp show such awareness – a state that probably comes with age, and from natural cunning, as well as from living in a clear, rich lake – that it is probably as well to consider the fish themselves in some minute detail. It is vital to realize that carp are living, breathing organisms that show great sensitivity to the watery world around them.

Harry Haskell has used the word 'trigger' to describe something that impinges on the carp's mental state and clicks it into some sort of action. This is how he explains it.

The word 'trigger' here means something that provokes or induces a reaction from a carp,

changing the *status quo*. Reactions to triggers vary from very mild and hardly perceptible to very violent and dramatic.

Triggers (stimuli) themselves may be something quite natural, like the sun coming up or going down, or unnatural, like you casting a bomb too close to a fish. Generally, naturally-occurring triggers, which may result in a carp feeding, resting, swimming, leaping, spawning and so on, are part of its everyday life and are mostly positive and acceptable. However, whilst man-made triggers can be positive, they more often prove negative.

Although not much is known in depth about this highly complex subject, we can draw a parallel with ourselves and with our own experiences, both on and off the bank. We can also assume that whatever the trigger is, it works via a message to the brain which, in turn, evokes a muscular reaction of some sort.

Another point of interest is that the reaction to a negative trigger is often instinctive, involuntary and violent. As a practical example, shout BOO! in your mate's ear next time he is dozing off. Conversely, the reaction by carp to a positive trigger is normally a much more sedate affair, unlike the true hunters – pike, trout and cats! A primary positive trigger both man-made and natural for the latter three is movement and whilst carp and other non-true hunters' reactions are normally positive to natural movements, they are definitely negative to man-made movements (although there are rare exceptions).

Of practical significance to our carping are the primary triggers: sound and movement (hearing), light and movement (vision), temperature, dissolved oxygen and so on (metabolism) and, finally, various stimuli of the olfactory, gustatory organs, hypothalamus, and indeed the whole brain nervous system, including the spinal cord. The trigger itself may comprise one of the above, but is most likely to be a combination. Also, as a trigger is an action, there will be a reaction on the carp's part which we, as anglers, can at best only observe in its physical form. I will leave you to draw your own conclusions as to the significance of the following basic notes regarding these triggers.

Sound and movement (vibrations/hearing) are detected via the hearing organ within the inner ear (lagena) and sensory cells located beneath and along the lateral line. It is understood that a carp has a wide acoustic range reception capability with the swim-bladder acting as an amplifier. In a dense medium like water sound travels great distances and may attract or repel.

Light and movement (vibrations/vision): as light waves are another form of vibration they are obviously detectable via the eyes. Carp have been said to have poor eyesight, but if good eyesight means the ability to detect light waves I believe that carp have good sight and furthermore that the range extends into the infra-red end of the spectrum giving them a degree of night vision. My non-scientific based opinion is derived from my own and others' experiences which have, in the main, been close-range reaction observation. These observations are not often explained by conclusions drawn by professionals dissecting eyeballs and counting rods and cones in a laboratory.

The carp's four sensitive barbules act as a sense of touch to detect physical movement and form, being primary over eyes when light levels are too low, for example when probing into silt for bloodworm. However, as far as I am aware, the eyes are primary over barbules when feeding mid-water.

Though light itself is another highly complex subject, simple available light levels are experienced triggers. I have yet to find a truly satisfactory explanation as to why decreasing or increasing light levels either trigger feeding or stop it. This is perhaps a little less marked for carp than other fish, though on some waters you can almost set your watch by it. Despite this, there are many contradictions which add to the confusion.

There are some carp in some waters which feed predominantly at night, some during daylight, and some both, and furthermore these feeding periods often change during the season.

Why is this? Perhaps the word 'feed' should be substituted with 'are caught'. Possibly genetics and water chemical make-up play a part. There also seems to be a difference between old silty ponds and hard-bottomed gravel/clay pits as far as bottom baits go, but this is only a generalization.

For several years I fished two Avon big winter roach swims. Swim one produced many two-pounders during frosty bright sunlight, although never after three o'clock in the afternoon, while just thirty yards away swim two was useless in even poor daylight, with feeding commencing at four o'clock (dusk), the more traditional time. Same fish just moving swims? It remained forever a conundrum.

Changing light levels are a primary trigger for roach and you, as a carp angler, will no doubt have experienced those infuriating sharp pulls on boilies at dawn and dusk, or perhaps the less urgent ones from your favourite friend, the bream! It is useful for a carper to know which is which.

Water temperature is the third primary trigger. Unlike us, fish are ectothermic, which means that their body temperature changes with that of their environment at about plus one degree above. If the water temperature is too high or low they tend to nod off. Their metabolism slows down and they become lethargic. The metabolism rate is influential on eating and digesting, they have, in fact, a 'demand and satisfy' which is linked to temperature.

There has been so much written about water temperature that I will not say more except this which is rarely mentioned. Although the range of possible feeding temperatures is wide, the optimum band is small, and at the point of fishing the demand/satisfy requirement may well differ with individual fish (theoretically it should always differ to some degree). As a generalization, a large old carp will require less pro rata than a young growing one, and it is worth remembering that a double or low twenty-pounder may be a very old fish and a thirty may be a relatively young one still growing.

A large Boathouse mirror.

Dissolved oxygen content is linked to temperature and vitally important to a carp's metabolism. A sudden and significant rise or fall provides a trigger and this change, apart from temperature, may be the result of external influences – wind, rain, pumped pollution – or internally within the water itself – decaying vegetation, algae, plant photosynthesis and so on.

Carp are well adapted to tolerate low dissolved oxygen levels, although they will cease to feed if levels drop too low or indeed become too high. I am unsure of the precise optimum band, but would guess at 4–5ml per litre, although within reason this preciseness is only of academic interest to the carper. On many summer waters, fishing into a fresh wind can bring in feeding fish, as can rain, although I know waters where it is the kiss of death.

Food itself is the fourth primary trigger. Simply all food, natural and man-made, give off chemical messages which, remember, are within the very solution in which carp live. Natural foods like bloodworm or maggots have the added attraction of movement. Man-made inert foods like your boilies tend not to move about, although they might have sight appeal. It would appear that the chemical messages derive from the emission of amino acids, detectable by the carp's taste and smell receptors.

The long-held belief of 'protein detection' is currently being investigated due to the anomaly of the 'background protein count' often found to be higher in natural waters than that possible from bait emission.

At first glance, this implies it would not be

possible for a carp to detect a bait by protein emission. Unfortunately, at the moment I do not have sufficient information relating to the specific density of 'background protein' found during recent tests.

There are several other triggers not mentioned, but a final one which may influence your catch rate is the greed/competitiveness factor. If you can accept that not all carp are the same, that they really have differing characters and traits, you will be in a much better position to understand and exploit the situation as and when it arises.

Fish are highly complex creatures and it is comforting to know that arrogant man cannot yet make one, nor for that matter even a humble maggot.

HIPPUS VULGARIS

The Water

An old estate lake of four to five acres, it lies in a shallow valley running roughly north-west to south-east. It is dammed at one end where the depth shelves to about five feet and tapers gradually to the reeds at the far end where the depth is only a few inches. The bottom is very regular with no real stream course through the middle as is so often the case with estate lakes. The water itself is generally very clear and is extraordinarily rich. Clouds of *Daphnia* throughout the warmer months cover the lake and there is no doubt that the carp browse extensively on this.

The Fish

The lake is controlled by a syndicate of very long standing that in the early 1970s had the foresight to dig a small lake beneath the dam, stock with small carp and rear on to a sensible size for release. As a result, the lake now contains probably fifty to sixty carp of mature years, ranging from perhaps mid-doubles to just into the thirties. These are super, original

estate lake fish with a beautiful, slim shape to them: every single one is a perfect target fish. Other species include tench, which once really flourished but have gone back steadily since the introduction and growth of the carp. There might also be some rudd still in existence; again, many years ago there were super shoals of these gorgeous fish to well over 2lb.

The Problem

The problem can be summed up in two words: *Hippus vulgaris*, or, to you and me, the common mare's tail. This weed is rooted in the mud and grows up to the surface, holding approximately six inches of its head proud. It has a coarse sinewy stem with spikey leaves that sit off it at right angles, and shows a small flower in the high-summer months. It appears to like slow-moving or preferably still water and can survive being totally submerged without suffering any set-back at all. So far, mare's tail seems quite an innocuous sort of weed and generally it is. At this particular lake, however, it has become completely out of control. If I remember rightly, back in the late 1960s there were small, isolated patches of the weed appearing in the shallows. I did not see the lake through the late 1970s or most of the 1980s and it was a shock in 1987 when I visited the lake again. The mare's tail had completely choked the entire water and there were only the tiniest of fishing patches here and there amongst it.

Not being a member of the club and only being allowed to visit it occasionally as a guest, there was very little that I could do apart from fish as opportunistically as possible. Accordingly, on the second journey I patrolled the lake until I saw a fish working fairly close to one of the clearings no more than a yard square. Sweetcorn appeared to do the trick and soon the bait was picked up, the float slanted away and a fish of, I guess, 12lb to 15lb was thrashing at the end. Not for long. The fish made a steady run into the mare's tail, zigzagged a couple of times and it was more than the 12lb line could bear. It came back frayed by the

Late summer and the weed has died down considerably.

rough weed stems and obviously had not stood a chance.

Enquiries revealed that hardly any fish were hooked from one season to the next and even those that were hooked were almost invariably lost.

This was confirmed on the next session when my partner, a member, hooked a fish which simply ran a couple of yards and became totally embedded. I began to strip, prepared to swim out for the fish, but it was no use: as before, the line quickly fluttered back, tattered beyond all use. Yards of it had to be cut away as quite useless after that thirty-second battle.

The Solution

So far there has not been one! My own visits to the lake slowed down and finally ceased alto-gether and I have not gone there again for at least five years. In the meantime, as far as I can gather, the amount of carp taken each season remains extraordinarily low. For example, during the 1992–1993 season, my information is that only three fish were landed.

The mare's tail still reigns supreme and simple dragging seems to have had little or no effect whatsoever. Indeed, the trouble with mare's tail, like Canadian pond weed, is that the more it is cut, the more spores it seems to shed and the more thickly it will return. The alternative is to treat the lake chemically and this the club has shied away from, partly for economical but also for environmental reasons. I, personally, am always a little wary of chemi-cal treatments as, from time to time, I have seen them go badly wrong and change the whole character of the water. At least here, despite

A carp from a heavily weeded water.

being very difficult to catch, the carp are happy, well fed and obviously enjoying life; it would be a shame to jeopardize this for the simple pursuit of our own pleasure.

I would like to think that if I were to fish there on a regular basis I would be able to wean the carp on to surface feeding. This, as far as I know, has not been tried seriously. Rich estate lake carp can be notoriously difficult to get to the top. Redmire is a case in point, and I found the same situation when I fished the Boathouse Lake. In all my time there I only hooked two fish on the surface. The same holds true at the lake we are now studying. The reluctance of carp to come to the surface here is emphasized by the openness of the water and the fact that there is generally some sort of wind chill on it. However, time, patience and perseverance could pay dividends and if a fish could be hooked on the surface, with the right gear, its head could possibly be held clear of

the water and it could be hustled from the bank before it had time to dive and make its way through the line-fraying mare's tail.

The second approach would be to concentrate on the comparatively free areas, bait these heavily and draw in as many fish as possible. Once the fish began to feed here with total lack of caution, it would be theoretically possible to go for them with extremely heavy tackle, line thick enough to repel a fair amount of abrasion and strong enough to stop a carp in its tracks and haul it to the bank – although I do not particularly like the effect this can have on a fish's mouth.

(This is another avenue of thought altogether, really; playing a big fish very heavily can cause mouth problems which none of us want to inflict. However, if sufficient pressure can be put on early enough in the fight it is quite possible to land a fish that hardly struggles in a completely bewildered daze.)

RICH WATER AND WEED-BEDS

The problem of heavy weed affects estate lakes throughout Great Britain and here is a challenge solved by Ian Jones from Wales who found a situation very similar to the one just described.

The Water

An estate lake of about four acres with depths of five or so feet shallowing to a matter of inches, the water is always very heavily weeded. The problem is a mixture of lilies and very thick Canadian pond weed which cloaks virtually the entire lake. The water is generally murky, but is very rich in all manner of food forms, including vast colonies of swan mussels. Silting is a major problem, exacerbated by excessive weed growth. Tench, roach, rudd, bream and perch make up the bulk of the other species in the lake.

The Fish

A few younger fish were stocked into the lake, but there are about fifteen large carp present as we approach the mid–1990s. These probably date from a stocking in the early 1960s, for Rod Hutchinson caught a nineteen-pounder from the lake in 1971. Today the maximum size is probably about 20lb: a 25lb common carp was recently caught, but most of the big fish appear to be mirrors.

The Problem

The problem has probably become all too clear: the richness of the water means that it is difficult to wean the fish off their natural food and on to any bait. The weed makes everything

A corner of Ian's lake.

Dave Plummer with a magnificent French mirror.

Gardener's Lake success.

(Opposite) *Ian Jones cracks his Welsh estate lake.*

An immaculate, lean estate lake fish.

A wild carp is released.

Weed – the nightmare.

Chris Ball with a superb surface-caught fish.

A superb carp taken from the surface by Chris Ball.

This mid-twenty caused John Bailey one of his worst ever headaches, and took over two days of constant stalking and plotting to put on the bank.

(Opposite) *Julian's pride.*

A carp from Wood Pigeons in the 1980s.

A Balkan carp held for the sunshine.

The magnificent mahseer.

A carp in the winter really can be something of a challenge: the bait, the approach, the swim and the time of attack must all be chosen with the greatest care.

Crucians taking bread from the surface.

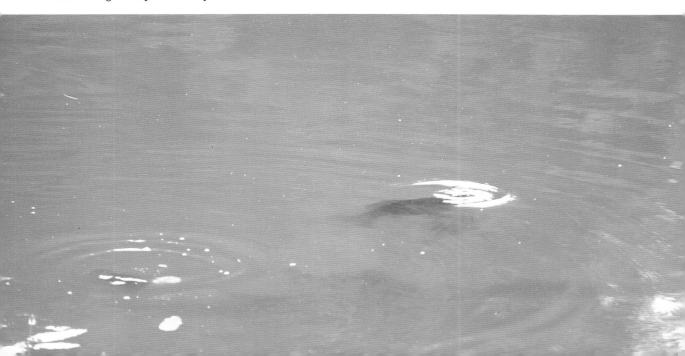

Just landing a fish with a tail like this is challenge enough!

Not a challenge yet . . . however, the parents of this fish, from a remote lake in Kashmir, weighed at least 40lb and totally defeated John Bailey.

Dave Plummer with a magnificent foreign common carp.

This was a particularly well fed fish from a very rich lake whose superabundance of naturals offered tough competition to anything from the bait larder.

(Opposite) *A lovely winter leather.*

A visible carp is frequently a catchable carp.

A fish does not have to be large to be appreciated or to be difficult.

Very often carp will spend the entire day in thick lily-beds and are only accessible during occasional sorties out into open water.

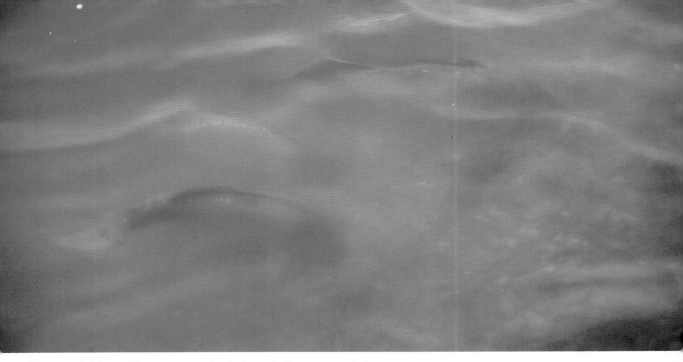

The sort of sight we all want to see: the challenge half-way to a solution.

Sunset over a weeded Welsh water.

Tony Miles cradles a Cassein monster.

Ian just shows what lilypads are made of.

more difficult and the carp do not seem to go into open water at all. Matches are held on the lake and channels are cleared for the competition anglers; these might attract tench but the carp are virtually never seen in them at all.

The Solution

Ian's solution (partial, he hastens to add, as he has hardly emptied the lake as yet) is a multi-layered one.

First, he fishes right into the weed-beds. The trick is to cut very small holes, no more than 2–3ft (60–90cm) in diameter. This necessitates the use of the club's punt and a 3ft (90cm) pronged drag that he made himself. The holes must be kept to this size, anything larger and the fish will simply not appear in them at all but avoid them with suspicion.

Tackle has to be very heavy for this sort of approach and Ian uses 15lb big game line, constantly aware that the lily roots are as thick as legs! He chooses a 2lb test curve through action rod which is quite soft; as it makes sense to cut the holes as close to the bank as possible, the rod must therefore be quite forgiving. He employs Owner hooks of a very heavy gauge (SSWs), size 6s are favoured. The hook is mounted on a light braid and Ian chooses The Edge, marketed by Rod Hutchinson, for its white flecked sections that merge nicely with the bed. The rig is a straightforward $1\frac{1}{2}$oz leger weight that is either semi-fixed or preferably sliding. The use of a bolt-rig in these sort of conditions is suicidal: upon being pricked, the carp simply charges off through the Canadian pond weed and retrieval is virtually impossible. The use of a confidence-rig is, therefore, preferable. As soon as the bite is signalled, it is vital to strike and get on top of the fish and, if at all possible, force its head up so that it cannot plough into the weed-beds all around the hole where it is hooked.

The successful bait has been tiger nuts. Boilies have simply resulted in enormous bags of tench, and other particles are again far from tench-proof. The tench will take tigers but not with any great relish. When campaigns have been successful, Ian has tried to make two visits a week to the water to keep a steady, small amount of tiger nuts going into each cleared area. These will preferably be laid over carpets of hemp.

Ian stresses the importance of dawn starts. First light and just before sees the peak of the carp's feeding cycle. This will continue longer on overcast days, especially if the night has been mild and overcast. If the night has been cold and clear and the sun rises bright and early, the inevitable feeding session tails off quite quickly.

The very biggest fish have eluded Ian so far, but I suspect this will not continue for very long. He has the bit between his teeth now and has developed a very successful approach to an extremely common form of challenge in estate lake carping.

A CHALLENGE AT WOOD PIGEONS

The Water

Wood Pigeons is, in fact, Holkham Hall Lake in North Norfolk. I gave it this false name when I wrote my first book *In Visible Waters* but now, for the sake of accuracy, I feel the truth should be told. I protected the lake's identity at that time because I feared an invasion by carp anglers, but now I realize such apprehensions were utterly groundless. Then, as now, the stock of fish in Holkham Lake and the restrictions placed upon fishing render the place useless for most weeks of the very short season there and I fail to see that any committed carp angler would take the place very seriously. However, I did many times over the years!

Holkham Lake is a strange water, some eighty to a hundred acres in size with varying depths from inches to six or seven feet at the dam end nearest the sea. The water is generally very clear and exceptionally rich, with enormous populations of *Daphnia* and water-fleas. There are islands dotted around the lake and weed growth can vary dramatically from year to year. The lake lies in a rough north to south axis and winds off the sea frequently comb it in the summer, bringing water temperatures down extremely rapidly.

The Fish

Herein lies one of the major problems (the others are that fishing is only allowed along a certain stretch of the bank, fishing stops in September, no night fishing is allowed and no fishing is allowed on Sunday!). The stock of carp is very low indeed and has been variously guessed at between fifty and a hundred fish; approximately, then, one fish per acre of water! Whether the carp are wildies or commons is also open to debate. My biggest fish actually landed went into low doubles and although I still regard it as my largest wildie I cannot be quite sure. Certainly, in the past there have

A classic Wood Pigeons common.

been two or three big fish into the twenties, which suggests that there is probably at least an influence of the common carp strain present.

The carp are exceptionally mobile and no such thing as a good swim really exists. However, there are times when a large percentage of the lake's population comes together for some particular reason, either around spawning or to exploit some exceptionally prolific food source.

There are few 'nuisance' fish. In the 1950s and early 1960s Holkham was a truly teeming lake with specimen perch, tench and roach, but something happened around 1965 or 1966 to thin stocks dramatically – to the point where they have never really been able to re-establish themselves. I have seen the occasional enormous tench and once caught a 2lb roach but both those events were back in 1979 and probably represented the last of their species. The decline has been blamed on effluent from the pottery factory or on an invasion of cormorants for two successive winters when up to three thousand birds inhabited the lake. Perhaps a combination of the two is to blame.

The Problem

I have probably already outlined enough problems to put most sensible people off and I only kept returning because I loved the lake and felt a true challenge existed. In 1986 a large number of the lake's carp had gathered about eighty yards from the sluice gates on the dam past the bottom island. I was fairly sure that something was going on by the number of carp that I saw topping during a couple of reconnaissance sessions. Eventually, with the aid of binoculars and the surrounding pine trees, I was able to establish that the fish were patrolling an area about the size of half a football pitch way out from the bank, which fortunately contained several large, clear sandy areas where a bait could be presented well. Quite why the carp had gathered in this area was at first beyond me – until I began to realize that the various wind currents had set up a *Daphnia*-drift around that particular area. I feel the carp were simply browsing through this liquid food bonanza. Considering this, I decided that particle baits would offer the best chance and settled for sweetcorn.

Very few anglers had fished the lake in earnest for carp and probably well under twenty per cent of the population had ever been hooked, so I felt that sweetcorn would be far from wasted. Also, a lake as old and traditional as Holkham hardly needs an invasion of boilies.

For a few days I prebaited with corn, frozen into handy-sized cubes that could easily be catapulted out to the largest area of clear sand that I had marked and lined up carefully. Close observation from my climbing tree revealed that most of the corn was landing fairly centrally. After four or five days of this, when I was quite confident that corn was being taken, I began to fish.

A view from the dam.

After two long sessions I was feeling very frustrated indeed. No matter what type of terminal rig or indication I used, all I was getting were a series of twitches with no proper runs developing. Obviously I struck at many of these twitches but nothing came back, apart from, on a couple of occasions, some fluttering scales. It all became extremely tiresome and worrying and I checked my various set-ups again and again but could find little fault with them.

It had probably been staring me in the face all along but it took me some twenty-eight hours of fishing time to realize. The corn, of course, was fished on a hair and I simply inserted a piece of polystyrene on to the top piece of corn and used a smaller hook so that the rig was semi-buoyant or at least neutral in weight. Immediately the bites became confident and runs unmissable.

the carp sucked so gently
the hook bait failed to rise

solution

hook packed with polystyrene
to achieve neutral buoyancy

The Wood Pigeons carp problem . . . and the solution.

Later in the week, I managed to get fish feeding quite close to me and it became apparent what was happening: the carp simply were not sucking with the customary vigour of the species. I tried fishing the old rigs where I could see what was happening and I realized that corn that was not buoyant was simply not being sucked up properly at all. In fact, the carp were going over a bed of corn sucking all the free offerings up and leaving the hookbait behind, not through wariness but simply because of their particular feeding behaviour.

I am not quite sure why the carp were feeding in this particular way at this particular time but I feel it possible that the conundrum had something to do with the *Daphnia* banks. Obviously the carp hardly had to suck at all as they wallowed through these beds of living food. Over some weeks perhaps they became conditioned to simply opening their mouths and doing little more than breathing in and the food would follow. Presumably they simply stepped up the sucking motion just a little to make sure that the corn went in but any corn heavier than usual was neglected. Obviously, I cannot swear that this was the case but it seems to me to be a good guess.

I rather like the moral behind this challenge for it reinforces something I have always believed in every branch of fishing: that every single little thing must be right or success will be severely limited. I believe that this applies just as much to shy canal roach or an educated chalk-stream trout as it does to any wily old

Patience at Wood Pigeons.

carp. One flaw in the set-up can result in complete and utter frustration. Harry Haskell picks up this point, underlining just how important it is to get everything right – especially on large waters where you cannot visually see what is going on. Just think, at a range of eighty or ninety yards, how many carp perhaps inspect your bait and you know little or nothing about it at the rod end. This is what Harry refers to as the 'enquiry', a term I like tremendously.

Rigs

We, as carpers, have to concede that we will and do need rigs. Indeed, the right rig or set-up, if you like, can increase our chances of converting an enquiry into a take and, rest assured, enquiries are more frequent than is indicated at the rod end of things, a statement which is substantiated by close range observation.

If we accept that a rig is generally considered to be that section of tackle from the lead down, including bait mounting, there are three basic, but vital prerequisites required, each being dependent upon the other to achieve a pick-up: location of a feeding fish, an acceptable bait, and an acceptable presentation. Rigs form a major part of presentation, so this is the area we will give much thought to.

Wishing to avoid pointless repetition by going over the same ground covered by others, such as Hutchinson, Maylin, Maddocks, Gibbinson and so on, I will concentrate on a few under-used rigs and materials. Kevin Nash's *Advanced Rig Book 88* is still very much worth a look at, although I would not recommend the untucked blood knot, nor the use of links and leads on three-way swivels (tethered fish).

Many, sometimes quite successful, carpers dismiss the need for rigs, other than the one, and only one, they use. Whilst there is a need to keep things simple, a restricted repertoire of presentation, invariably requires compensating factors, this usually being time.

Flexibility

A friend of mine who has caught a few very large carp has become somewhat stereotyped due to the aforementioned factors. To date the equation of relating potential = fish × time is not in balance. This previous success has resulted in a tendency to use one basic set-up and a commonly shared perception: 'If I'm not getting any action, the carp aren't feeding or here, and if I do stick one it sure won't get away.' Advanced carpers realize that the reward of stagnant thinking is silence.

Mr X's basic rig invariably comprises one or two 18mm ready-mades, dental floss hair off the shank via black tubing, size four Drennan SS hook, 12in 12lb Silkworm link, a black 2oz bomb mounted on a long length of black anti-tangle tubing, plus 12lb main line, all pulled up tight with monkeys. This set-up is similar to the ones most widely used for some years

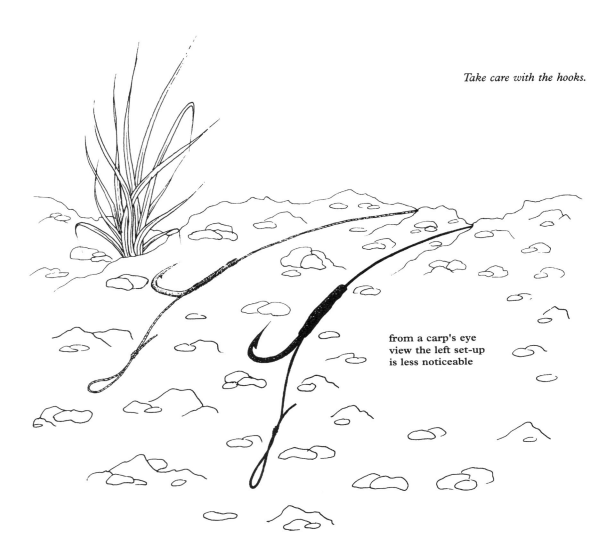

Take care with the hooks.

from a carp's eye
view the left set-up
is less noticeable

and will no doubt ring a bell with you and the carp!

As an illustration and to test Heavy Metal, Magma and Hawser, I fished on numerous occasions against my friend's set-up just to confirm that correct application of the above products, attention to detail and flexibility of presentation at the point of fishing, really would result in increased bobbin activity.

Using two fairly easy daytime doubles waters we sat side by side, fishing over the same swim using his ready-mades. In every case we apparently had more action than any other carpers. The simple, yet finely tuned rigs resulted in a dramatic increase in pick-ups. Typical was 2–4, 3–5, 3–6, 5–9 and, the final and best result, a 3–10!

The conclusion that may be drawn from this, is that although my friend should have had on average the same number of enquiries as myself, often in that crucial, final second on the part of the carp to make the commitment, it aborted. Or to put it simply, more often than not the rig proved too crude and was unacceptable. Flexibility is a crucial asset to any angler, it is folly to rely on luck only. We all need a spoonful of luck sometimes, but you cannot be lucky all the time. Dogma is the glue which will stick your monkeyclimbers, believe me. I get stuck up enough and realize I get it wrong more times than I get it right. The solvent solution is usually a self-analysis of what you are trying to achieve and how you are trying to achieve it.

My own rig, or rather rigs, in the previous mentioned testing, consisted simply of using Silk-worm braids 8/10/12lb between 5 to 10in (12–25cm) length, treated with one or two drops of Magma liquid tungsten to topple the link over, thus making it lay down, but with some give. A split floss hair was finely whipped and coated with Hawser to the shank of a 10/8/6 Drennan SS colour-blended hook. The hair came away off the shank in line with the point,

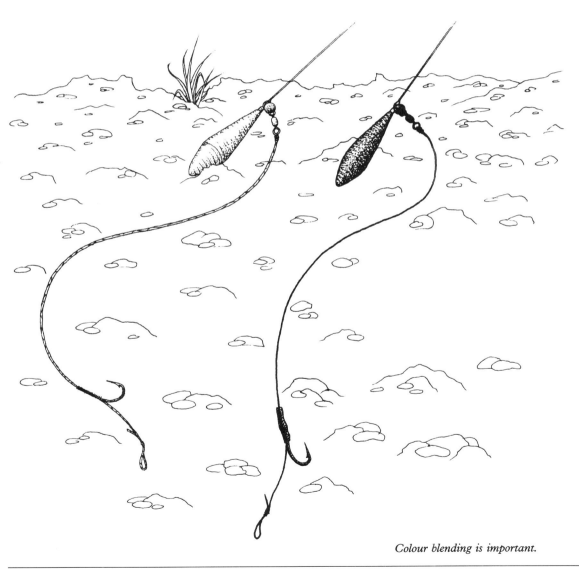

Colour blending is important.

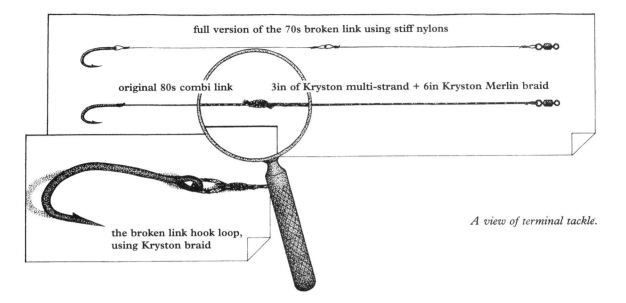

full version of the 70s broken link using stiff nylons

original 80s combi link

3in of Kryston multi-strand + 6in Kryston Merlin braid

the broken link hook loop, using Kryston braid

A view of terminal tackle.

either from the top or side opposite the offset.

The swivel and running bombs 1½/2/2½oz were also colour blended with the main line either 8 or 11lb, which was then pinned down 12in (30cm) and 30in (76cm) back from the lead with two small sausages of Heavy Metal. Did I say simply? It is, but requires some thought, it is about fine tuning, fineness and making every effort to negate the tethered factor, last-second abortion, and spooking by association. That is simple enough, isn't it?

As you will have noted, my set-up is in reality only complex in its versatility. The waters mentioned comprised a gravel pit carrying some suspension and a sand pit with gin-clear water. Having the ability to tie really neat hairs via whipping and Hawser resin, laying down a buoyant hook-link with Magma, pinning the main line down behind the lead or colour blending individually may well give you an extra chance.

A combination of all the above plus the right hook, bait, length of hair and link all in the right spot on the right day will give you several extra pick-ups. To reiterate, the key is fineness, tuning and balance of presentation even when using what is a basic rig.

THE GARDENER'S LAKE

There is a mistaken belief that carp fishing is somehow superior to other branches of angling. I have already said that I believe all fish are capable of learning surprisingly quickly, even the small species, the so-called nuisance fish. Tench fishermen, chub fishermen, matchmen all have to stay a step ahead of the game and constantly ring changes or make refinements. It is a shame that some carp anglers fish for carp only and fail to appreciate other species, other pleasures and other challenges.

Having said that I will agree that carp are pretty well top of the intelligence ladder – and I do mean intelligence in a sense that we can understand and appreciate as humans. After years of observation, I do not feel that carp simply show a conditioned reflex to the problems that confront them. My own feeling is that carp show a real ability to work things out and make decisions on the evidence of what they have seen. I think we do wrong if we underrate their reasoning power.

Let me start by giving a strange example. This very short story is of twenty-three cockerels. They live, or lived, over the walled garden

Astonishingly fertile . . . and difficult to fish.

a few yards from my house. The problem was that with that number of cockerels the dawn chorus was simply deafening and you have no idea how tiring it is to wake every single morning at about four o'clock to volleys of noise.

On one particular evening, a misguided cockerel decided to camp out in the fig tree below my bedroom window. Sure enough, as the first gleam of light cracked in the east, the cockerel began to sing out to its friends. To have the bird only feet from the bedhead was more than I could stand and, shuffling out into the half light, I managed to put a ladder up to the tree and seize the creature by the neck. Its life was in the balance, but would have been saved if it had not looked me in the eye and given a defiant cock-a-doodle-doo. So good was it that a few days later when I saw a cockerel strutting around the garden without a care

in the world I managed to corner it and had it for supper.

So far so good, and I began to think that I would cut down quite significantly on the shopping bill. Not so; after those two assassinations, whenever a cockerel saw me it would immediately leap on to the dividing wall and fly off with a last defiant mocking crow. The death of just twelve per cent of their comrades had made an immediate, indelible impression. To me, this is reasoning and not conditioned reflex; after all, the neck stretching had not happened to them personally and it was doubtful if more than a very few had even witnessed what had happened. Still, the word had got round and the cockerels had drawn their own conclusions.

At exactly the same period, I was experiencing a similar situation at a local estate lake.

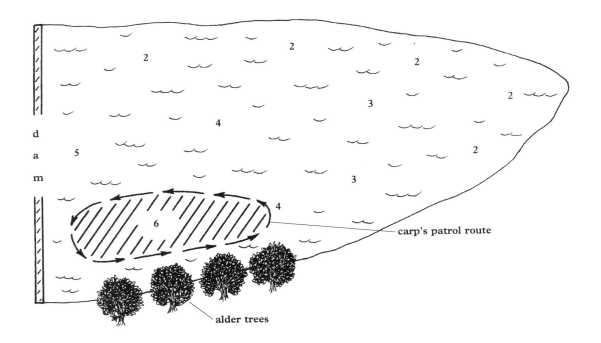

carp's patrol route

alder trees

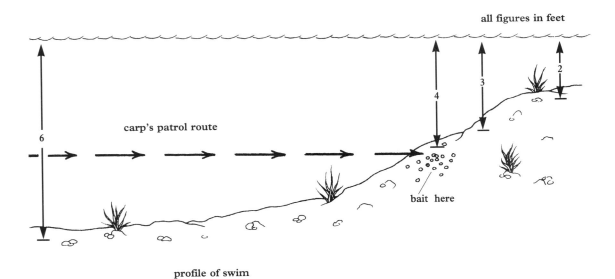

all figures in feet

carp's patrol route

bait here

profile of swim

The Gardener's Lake.

The Water

The Gardener's Lake is somewhat less than one acre with depths ranging from six or seven feet at the dam to a matter of inches in the shallow end. It is nearly always crystal clear and is only open to the north as trees shelter it on the other three sides of the valley. It is very much an underfished estate lake, dug about one hundred and ten years ago. The bottom is predominantly gravel and sand covered in most places with a layer of silt. There are just nine carp in the water and precious little else apart from a few eels. Five of the nine fish are around 20lb or just over and there is one that is much larger and probably approaches the mid-thirties. The water is very rich indeed. The weed virtually chokes it in the summer and it rarely dies off fully in the winter but remains at a level

that is average for most summer waters. The food stocks are incredibly high: not only do the winter months see whole blankets of *Daphnia*, but there is every type of insect that any pocket book can identify and in the evening the hatches of midges are just extraordinary. The pool is basically spring-fed, which keeps the temperatures down in certain areas but a stream also trickles into the southern, shallow end. There are particularly good fish-spotting trees on the west bank, old alders with very obliging branches.

The Target Fish

Any of the big five would have satisfied me in that particular period. These had probably been born in the water and were certainly twenty or more years old according to the

A beautiful Gardener's lake fish.

An earlier success at Gardener's Lake.

owner. He had a personal knowledge of them from at least the early 1970s. The five generally formed a small, integrated group which travelled in a loose fashion together. The four smaller fish in the water were probably later stockings; a rather haphazard introduction, for the water is rather too cold for successful spawning. (Although I am not saying they could not be the fruits of an especially successful and warm summer.)

The biggest fish of all has been caught once and possibly twice in the past eight years. Other fish have been hooked from time to time but often lost because of the weed. During this eight-year period at least three different larger fish have been landed, all around the 20lb mark. Fishing pressure is very light and these cannot possibly be regarded as neurotic fish. They are, however, very beautiful, with colours

just as rich as one would expect from such a clear, fertile water. Virtually all the carp are leathers, with just one or two scattered scales here and there, generally around the tail root.

In the summer the larger carp tend to hang in holes that they have made for themselves in the weed. There is a little movement at dusk and during the night but even this tends to be restricted during the high summer. There simply seems to be enough food in small areas of water to sustain them without them having to travel. In the winter, however, things change dramatically and the carp spend most of their time from October onwards in a slow drift around the pool. It is noticeable that most of their time is spent in the western corner of the dam and in the deep water on the west bank underneath the alders. This favoured area is probably about fifty yards in length and they frequently drift out towards the middle before returning, quite tight into the bank.

The Problem

My record on the Gardener's Lake is abysmal and I have only landed one of the big fish and that a good while ago in 1989. The problems in the summer are horrendous given the weed and the virtual immobility of the fish. For long periods of time there is almost complete pre-occupation with *Daphnia* and this decided me on a winter campaign.

Problems continue to abound in the winter as the water is still very fertile and at least as clear as it is in the summer. The period that I chose to fish was very dry and there was not even the rain that could have tinged the water a little. There were also occasional frosts which killed what was left of the algae and made the water, if possible, even more crystal.

There was no one else on the water or even walking around it. This made the fish that much more sensitive to any bankside movement. Also, the trees were bare and the grass and the weed growth generally down so that little cover was available. The carp, as a result, soon showed very strong signs of being aware of my presence within minutes of my arrival at the water. Obviously, I countered this by approaching the water as carefully as I possibly could, certainly from areas that gave me some backdrop of trees and, once in position, by moving as little as possible.

Corn had not been used on the water for years and I prebaited with it for a week. From my position in the alder trees I could see that this was being accepted and I decided to fish during the afternoons. I chose a float rig (for no other reason really than I like to use one) and a size ten hook with two grains on, all fished in close to the bank. In a nutshell, one fish was hooked and lost under a sunken branch and two other fish were pricked. The result was devastating. From my alder tree perch I saw over the next four days that the corn was totally ignored. More than that, it was being actively avoided. The wandering group of carp would make a wide circuit around it. All the fish that is, not just simply the ones that had had a nasty experience.

The weather grew colder and the fish movements slowed down and became confined to the deepest water under the alder branches themselves. I began to introduce some boiled baits – I cannot remember what flavour and it is not really important; all I can say is that they were a dark red. The carp did begin to feed on them but I had to fish from the alder branches themselves to put any bait down. It was impossible to cast into this particular hole from the other bank because of the still quite vibrant weed.

It was immediately obvious that the fish were afraid of the float and the line hanging in the water and they gave both a very wide berth. It appeared obvious on the second session that they were also, somehow, aware of me above them even though I tried to merge as tightly as possible to the quite thick trunk of the tree. From this time, the carp stopped eating the boilies. They stopped moving and simply sulked just beneath mid-water. This particular approach was obviously at an end.

The Solution

I decided to move back to particles, to tiger nuts. I believed that the carp had never been happy with the boiled baits and that particles are much more like a natural food, and something they are accustomed to. For a whole week, I visited the water quickly and quietly to prebait only. I would cautiously climb the tree to ensure that the nuts were going and, after only the first baiting, I was quite sure that they were.

I began to concentrate on one particular area at the end of the patrol route, tight under the last of the alder trees. This, I believe now, was critical. In part, this last alder tree gave the patrolling fish shade and security. The other crucial factor is that the bottom began to shelve quite deeply here and any mid-water travellers

A fascinating shot of carp spawning in an estate lake.

would find themselves face to face with the bottom and food. It was a small, critical area. It was much easier to cast two yards to the right but, by then, the carp had left the bottom and were chewing any baits that they had found. They would also meet the line and the float and this unsettled them and made them very much disinclined to go down and feed again.

Another problem emerged: how would I get a bait on this exact patch that was now uncovered of silt by the constant attention the fish were giving it? There were willows immediately to the right once the alders petered out, only giving me the tiniest of fishing positions. I would have to cast over the willows into the middle of the lake and draw the bait back under the alder tree and let it settle in the exact place. This manoeuvre would have to be done quickly to stop the terminal gear sinking down in the water and picking up weed on the retrieve. For

that reason a heavy bomb was quite impossible, for it would simply act as a weed drag. Two swan shot were quite heavy enough to make the cast and yet light enough to be pulled over the weed without sinking in and cloaking the bait. The float also had to go – much as I like to use one, it obviously stood out like some sort of lighthouse to these wary fish in such clear water. I took no chances at all; the first length of dacron was coloured black so that it would lie as invisibly as possible upon the dark silt and weed. A couple of feet from the hook, I coloured it a mottled brown and white so that it would lie inconspicuously over the emerging sand and gravel.

On the eighth day, after a week of prebaiting, I put a handful of nuts around this critical area and made my first proper cast. I could see the nuts on the hair clearly on their way back from the middle of the lake. I allowed them to flutter down and to lie as centrally in the clear area as

A floater bait was successful this time.

I could. I let the line hang slack so that it too would settle on the bottom as naturally as possible.

After a couple of hours the group of five fish appeared from my left, from underneath the alders. I pressed myself back into what undergrowth there was. The fish obviously stopped over the baited area and a couple of them tipped up to take in some food. The fish then moved off.

An hour and ten minutes later the group of fish returned. The same thing happened, apart from one good fish remaining behind. It hung around the baits for ten minutes and I could see that it was picking up occasional food by the flash of its flank as it altered position. Finally, the bobbin jumped, the fish moved and the bobbin rose all the way. That, at last, was that: no mistakes on the way to the net and I was holding a very treasured prize.

As an interesting postscript, I revisited the lake over the next three days to ensure that the fish was happy and to compare it with its brothers or its sisters. The nuts that had been left after the capture remained uneaten. Once again, the message had been transmitted around the pool.

Those who would dispute that carp have a recognizable intelligence would do well to think about the way this small group of fish faced problems and reacted so quickly, even though for much of the time nothing happened to them personally.

4 CARPING ABROAD

Although British anglers have fished spasmodically for carp on the Continent and further afield for many generations, the boom time only really began from the late 1970s and early 1980s. Suddenly, almost overnight it seemed, British anglers woke up to the fact that huge carp existed across the Channel and could sometimes be caught far more easily than those at home from smaller, heavily pressured waters. Cassein blazed the trail and even today has its own magic as a sort of Continental Redmire, but there are many other waters and different water types scattered around the globe that British anglers have investigated. Now, in the mid–1990s, British carpers have caught fish from the United States, from northern Africa, from all over Europe and from Australia. There are also the strange carp varieties and mighty mahseer to be found in Asia. The world, obviously, is the carp fisher's oyster.

Most carp fishing takes place in Europe where there are many types of water. Cassein is one type: a very large, deep, man-made lake covering thousands of acres where the fish population is not great and location and feeding patterns are extremely important. Then there are the smaller, more traditional old waters that dot France in particular, but can be found throughout Europe. Indeed there is one area of the Loire Valley which seems to be more carp ponds than land. Then there are the rivers and the canals of Europe that seem to hold far more carp of large sizes than do our own, the Trent, possibly, excluded. A serious travelling carp angler cannot afford to ignore the big European rivers or the canals of the Low Countries where commons, in particular, grow to enormous sizes. All this travelling has

also led to the development of purpose-built carp waters that cater for the English angler who would otherwise be a little unsure of where to start. Not very exciting, but still good enough for those who do not want to run before they can walk – and after all, not everybody wants to be a pioneer.

There has been some debate about whether foreign carp 'count'! This is one of the more ridiculous discussions in angling for, surely, a carp is a carp wherever it is caught. Some people prefer to stay at home and others wish to travel and, believe me, any thought that foreign carp are easy should be banished at once. Frequently, simply finding a carp water where carp fishing is allowed is challenging enough, never mind catching one! It can be very intimidating to be stuck many miles from home in a foreign land with money running out with a broken-down car and still not a run to call your own. It is enough to make you wish that you had stayed on the local park pond!

Some tremendous challenges remain abroad. The race for the first hundred-pound carp is on in some quarters and I have spoken to European anglers in particular who see this as a quite viable goal. Indeed, in all probability, a fish of this weight was even stocked into Cassein at one stage and it is very likely that one or two waters in the Mediterranean area hold fish of this sort of calibre. I have not seen them myself, but one or two reliable witnesses have spoken of immense fish. Then there is the thrill of discovering a completely unknown, untapped carp water, and, believe me, there are scores of these still to be found in parts of rural France alone. Eastern Europe remains almost totally unexplored apart from the very occasional pioneering trip by men such as Andy Little. Let me tell you of the carp I saw around the Caspian Sea during a recent trip there after sturgeon: there were commons in those brackish lagoons that really would have made anything, and I mean anything, that Redmire has produced seem trivial. And, as far as I am aware, a British carper has never even sniffed the area.

My own particular favourites are the mahseer, those huge carp-barbel of Asia. Is it right to include mahseer in a carp book? I believe so, after all the species are related and the venerated carp magazines sometimes run articles on them – proof, if anything, that the species is accepted! If we accept that mahseer are fair game for the carp angler a whole new world is opened up. As I write in 1993, virtually all the British mahseer fishing is carried out on the River Cauvery. There are good reasons for this: camps are fairly well organized and an angler does not, in reality, have to be particularly pioneering to get there and to succeed. I am not belittling fishing in southern India, but there is far more to mahseer fishing than these few short stretches. The whole of Asia holds mahseer and the size to which they may grow is unknown. There are mahseer (or very close relatives) in Pakistan, Bhutan, Ladakh, Nepal, Burma, Bangladesh, Thailand, Vietnam and even Sri Lanka, not to mention those similar fish of the Middle East that possibly still inhabit the waters of Iraq and Iran. In short, anybody who thinks that they know more than ten per cent of what there is to know about mahseer is a fool or totally self-deluded.

Phil Thompson, one of the new breed of carp giants, holds a wonderful fish from a big foreign water.

For anybody wanting to find carp abroad, apart from those in stocked lakes, the challenges are immense: first of all you have to find the water and arrange the fishing; then you have to locate the fish – often a very difficult task on very big waters; then you have to arrange a successful baiting programme; and finally you have to put the fish on the bank – often very difficult with carp way beyond all previous knowledge or even expectations. Anybody, therefore, who denigrates foreign carp because they do not have the courage or the desire to fish for them should be ignored. Foreign fish, especially if you have found them yourself, are a massive achievement – never let anybody say otherwise.

RUMOURS PROVED

Dave Plummer is possibly Britain's most successful French carp angler and has for several years conducted many tours of British anglers with unbelievable successes. However, it should not for a moment be thought that a rod and line in France guarantees success. Far from it. There invariably has to be a great deal of research, trial and effort, pain and tears before the leviathans finally wallow to the net. This tale describes one of his trips that could easily have ended in failure.

The year was 1989 and Dave and his travelling partner Richard Furlong were fishing at Salagoue near Montpellier in the south of France. They had landed fish to over 30lb, including commons, but became fired by rumours of a huge water with even larger fish present. However, all these were at this stage were rumours.

The Water

In 1989 St Quoix was not the famous water it is now. Dave and Richard were staggered by its vastness – even the bays were hundreds of acres. The lake is near Cannes and high in the mountains. In fact, it is late May and June before the water warms sufficiently to give much sport. Just knowing where to begin would prove to be a major headache.

The Fish

Let me emphasize again that there was no concrete proof of carp in St Quoix at that time as far as Dave and Richard were concerned. On their first trips around the lake no other carp anglers could be seen and even the local tackle dealers only talked about trout, perch and pike.

The Problem

Enough of the problem has probably been outlined, but remember that it took half a day for the pair to drive round the lake, near despair, never seeing a carp angler or a carp. Those of you who have seen these enormous European waters will know exactly the sinking feeling the two felt, but it is to their credit that they continued, made an attempt and finally found a solution.

The Solution

At last Dave and Richard found a bay behind an island that seemed to offer both shallows, depths and spawning areas. Close by was a camp-site into which they booked so that they were only five minutes away from the swims that they fancied.

They found that from the bank they could fish easily into fifteen to seventeen feet of water where they hoped they would intercept carp as they moved from the depths into the shallows. The first two days passed without anything untoward happening, certainly at the rod-end of things. However, little by little, Dave realized that there were carp in front of them, rolling very strangely. These fish behaved exactly like trout nymphing, that is in a slow, gentle porpoise-like motion. They were not acting in any way like the carp of Salagoue or Cassein that leap out with a resounding splash. Indeed, the pair had to watch the exact spot to see that the fish responsible were carp at all. Finally, one nymphed straight in front of Dave and there was no doubt that this was a very big fish indeed. Runs, however, still failed to materialize.

The pair were still without any action whatsoever by the third morning and were beginning to think that perhaps they had hit the water too early and that the water was too cold. They even debated moving down to Cassein. It was then that a French angler pulled up, pumped up an inflatable boat, rowed it out to within two or three hundred yards of them, dropped over bucketfuls of maize and returned to the bank. He was back into his car and off before they could say a word. The angler returned around tea-time, set up two hundred and fifty yards from Dave and within an hour landed a 34lb carp! At that moment, our heroic pair decided to stop!

On the fourth morning two more anglers moved into the bay beneath Dave, about half a mile away – such is the size of a French bay. Now there were four anglers on about seven thousand acres of water. The wind was blowing hard from Dave and Richard into the shallows near the French anglers who were fishing in five or six feet of water. That morning the Frenchmen landed ten fish in all, the biggest weighing 43lb 8oz, 38lb and 37lb, with commons to 28lb. It was truly unforgettable action.

The French pair suggested that Dave and Richard move beneath them, deeper down into the bay. Dave decided this would be beneficial and they moved their gear three to four hundred yards beneath the French and out on to a peninsula. Their confidence, now, was high and that evening they put two markers, a hundred yards out from the bank, around sixty or seventy yards apart. Around these markers they put out every last bit of bait they possessed: peanuts and boilies totalling about 330lb (150kg)! Richard was rather apprehensive about this bombardment, but Dave felt that the numbers and the size of the carp warranted it. Just before dark and packing-up time Dave hit into a 31lb 8oz mirror and their spirits

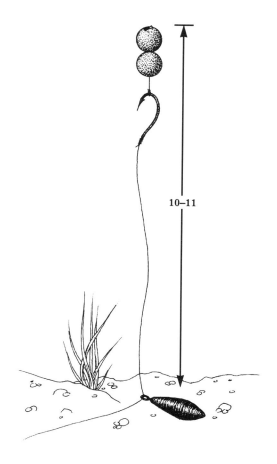

Dave Plummer's pop-up rig.

rose even further. It seemed that the mystery of St Quoix was about to be solved.

On the fifth morning, Dave and Richard moved into the swims at first light, about half past three. The three French anglers had gone back to Paris, a good day's drive away. There was not a ripple on the water and not a bubble from a fish. Nothing. The pair felt deflated, desperate even, sure that they had over-baited and overfaced the carp as a result.

Dave cast out his first rod which had two boilies popping-up about ten or eleven inches off the bottom. His second rod was cast out with a boilie on the bottom and he was about to put out a third rod with maze when the first rod was away! With a 34lb 8oz fish in the net, the second rod began to cry out. A hectic fight in and out of the weed-beds and a 44-pounder was landed! That fish had demanded that they take the boat to it and on the way back over the markers they saw, in the 8ft deep, gin-clear water, that every scrap of bait had gone. Yet the carp remained looking for anything that had not been sucked up. That morning Dave was to land another nine fish (eleven in all), all over 30lb. Richard, just by his side, landed a single fish of 15lb. That, though, Richard would be the first to accept, is fishing!

There are several aspects to this story: firstly, the pair took a gamble and acted simply on a hunch and scraps of information. This takes some courage when you are a couple of days away from home and money needs to be justified. Secondly, the pair showed their experience in choosing that particular bay that they felt would offer the depths the fish desired and was facing the prevailing wind. Thirdly, Dave showed the necessary bravery to put in all their bait in that one 'do-or-die' effort. This is often the way with Continental fish: they are big and they are greedy and they demand nothing less than one hundred per cent. Half-measures nearly always end in failure.

ONE FOR BOSNIA

The Water

The lake is a huge one situated just outside Biograd in what was Yugoslavia. In all, I guess the lake to be about four or five miles long and a mile in width. When I fished there it was clear but with an opaque tinge to it, probably a result of the infiltration of sea water that also made it slightly brackish to the taste. This infusion of salt did not seem to harm the natural life of the lake and certainly the carp did very well indeed on natural food. As to the depth of the lake, I really would not like to say but certainly when swimming and boating I frequently found areas of twenty feet or more.

There are several other species of fish in the lake, most notably enormous catfish, large pike and various other species of white fish.

The Fish

The carp are, generally, long, slim, fully-scaled common carp that could pass quite easily as wildies. However, there are some mirror carp in the water so it is doubtful whether the pure, ancient genetic strain has been preserved. It is very hard to estimate the numbers of fish in the lake; there are large areas pretty well denuded of them, whereas in other places good catches can sometimes be expected. Equally, it is very hard to be precise as to size; most of the fish that I saw tended to be on the small side and the very biggest that I witnessed was around fifteen to eighteen pounds. However, I do have it on good authority that thirty-pounders, although quite rare, are present in the lake. The problem for every carp is that the locals eat nearly everything they catch, and obviously to live to any age whatsoever a carp has to be particularly wary or very lucky.

The Problem

My problem was, simply, that I could not catch any fish! Corn seemed to be a very popular bait and I had brought a fair amount of it with me. It seemed quite easy at first to select a good-looking pitch, put in a marker some forty to sixty yards from the bank and swim out on a regular basis to distribute corn from a large tin. Then, it was back to the bank, sit by the rods and generally relax and dry out in the glowing sunshine. However, that is nearly all I did – relax! Every now and again the Optonics would bleep and a line would twitch, but that was about it. Once, when I had left the rods to investigate a commotion down the bank, I did return to find chaos. The carp had obviously chosen an opportune time to make a mistake and had got away scot-free – as it deserved to. For a few days I sat it out like this without making any inroads whatsoever into the local

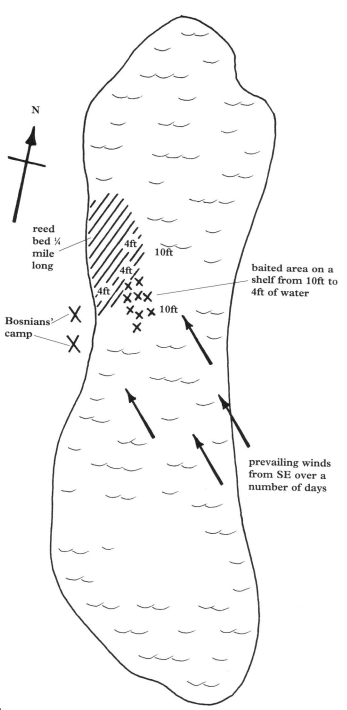

N

reed
bed ¼
mile
long

4ft
10ft

4ft

4ft

baited area on a
shelf from 10ft to
4ft of water

Bosnians'
camp

10ft

prevailing winds
from SE over a
number of days

A Bosnian carp lake.

The classic shape of a fully-scaled wild carp; the Balkans are full of such fish.

carp population. It did not really matter, though: the sun and the life-style were more than adequate compensations.

The Solution

The solution was not really mine at all and, as I have said, my own success rate remained pretty low. I must take my hat off to a family who fished forty or fifty yards away from me up the bank, resident on the shores of the lake for the duration of their holiday from Sarajevo. Altogether the family comprised six: mother, father and four angling-mad sons, all teenagers between twelve and seventeen. The family was a pure delight to fish with and many was the glass of wine and meal that we shared over the days. They were obviously there to enjoy themselves and the family holiday meant a very great deal to them.

The family's tackle was cheap and basic: short, bean-pole type rods with tiny fixed-spool reels that you had to crank crazily to retrieve any line at all. I say fixed-spools, for there were only two of those and the rest were antique centrepins of a model I had never seen before. Line, too, was of the clumsiest, most unreliable sort, and I was not too sure either about the make of hooks. Still, they sharpened them to a fine point and were never let down. The rigs, surprisingly, were about as up-to-date as any carp angler would expect to find at Savay! Hair-rigs and bolt-rigs, I was told, were nothing new to the Bosnian fishermen and had been passed down, father to son, for generations!

However, what made the family far more successful than I was their baiting programme. In short, the family loaded their swim with bait over the fortnight that they were there. Corn was the basis but, really, anything would do. Every scrap of left-over food from meals would be piled in along with anything else that the family could find along the shores of the lake, in the town or anywhere else. At one point, I seem to remember, they even found some left-over chicken meal that was rowed out in their inflatable boat and poured over by the sackful. The result of this extraordinary baiting was, I suppose, predictable: results steadily built up and soon hardly half an hour would go by without one of the family being into action of some sort. A missed bite, a lost fish, a thrilling battle (considering the tackle) and often a fish landed and barbecued before you could say Jack Hilton!

The lesson here is quite an obvious one and ties up with Dave Plummer's experience at St Quoix. Simply, on these very large Continental waters you must get the baiting right and frequently this involves a very large-scale operation indeed. The problem that many English and visiting anglers face is that they can deposit a mass of bait in totally the wrong place and ruin the entire chances of their holiday in one fell swoop. It is essential, therefore, to weigh-up very carefully the chosen swim and not to make any error whatsoever. If that is possible!

At the end of that holiday, the family went home with pleas for us to follow and a few days later we met them at their flat in Sarajevo. We were showered with the most tremendous hospitality – far more than a relatively poor family can afford I am sure, but they would not hear of stinting or cutting back in any way. A more generous, affectionate family it would be impossible to imagine and I shudder to think about what has happened to them and their loving life in the disasters that have befallen that sad city.

WHEN IS A CARP NOT A CARP?

A big fish is often not particularly difficult to hook, but the actual landing of it can be nearly impossible. Sound tackle is vital but so is skill, quick thinking and, sometimes, bravery – as in this case. This particular challenge was set by a mahseer, the carp-barbel of Asia. In the water the fish looks more like a barbel; held in the

sun it could be taken for a long, glittering common with a particularly large head and massive fins. The habits of the mahseer are something of a mixture of the two species. The fish is happy to feed off the bottom like a barbel or on the surface like a true carp. Although the mahseer is strongly predatorial, that does not mean that it will not take paste, crabs or really anything that it finds edible. In my own view the mahseer is enough like a carp to merit its place in this book. I have included this account as an example of what can be done in the most exacting conditions. The message is, when you are attached to a fish that you hardly know how to control, to stay calm and never, never give up. The hero of this story is, by the way, most definitely not me.

The Fish

I found myself attached to a mahseer of between 60 and 70lb. The fish could not be weighed properly as I did not have a stringer with me to secure it on and there was no way of keeping it alive till we got back to camp and found some scales. The mahseer was of the golden variety; in the south there are silver, black and green.

The Water

The river in question was the Cauvery in southern India, in Karnataka, somewhere between Bangalore and Mysore.

The Problem

The fish had hammered into a 5in silver spoon on 25lb line in a long, streamy pool some way up from the camp. I had actually been pulled over by the ferocity of its take and had never been able to exert any real pressure, let alone dominance. As a result, the mahseer had made its way steadily to the tail of the pool, where it had teetered, its fins erect and scales shining for a full five seconds before crashing into the maelstrom of water that emptied down a full

Not a carp but of the same family, nearly!

half-mile of rocks and waterfalls. These falls were breathtaking in their savagery before they emptied out into a large lagoon-like pool.

Viewed from below, the falls were simply a ladder of white water punctuated by great rocks and fallen trees. Deep channels, underwater currents and the relentless force of the water made any entry there seem like potential suicide. Once the mahseer had disappeared over the lip of the pool, the force of the water took it inexorably downriver. The rod was virtually pulled from my hand and, naturally, I felt that the whole battle was all over.

The Solution

Happily, my guide in the midday heat was Suban. Suban is a small, wiry, vastly experienced Indian. In some ways he is more otter than man and has made his living for many years helping idiots like me to catch their dreams – and he was not for letting this fish go. 'Swim. Swim sir. Swim. In. In. In.' I do not know why Suban tended to repeat every instruction two or three times but the effect

was galvanizing and in I went, following the Indian's bobbing black head down the rapids.

Almost immediately I became aware that the fish was now immobile and that there was no give in the line whatsoever. Not that I really cared; simply keeping my balance in such a flood of water on a narrow rock ledge surrounded by deep water was quite enough for my own concentration. Suban, however, had different ideas. He got hold of the line and followed it to where it met the water and dived. I swear that he was down a full minute before coming up. The mahseer, it appeared, had gone a complete circuit round a vast rock and was lying tethered ten yards beneath it. Suban pulled me to the great boulder so that I was half swimming, half struggling and half drowning. Finally I stood there, wedged to the boulder's top by the force of the water while Suban dived down again. He came up holding my broken line – to one end of which the mahseer was still attached! He broke my own line beneath the rod tip and tied, in a trice, a superbly strong water knot. Meanwhile, I held the fish on that short length of line to give him some slack to

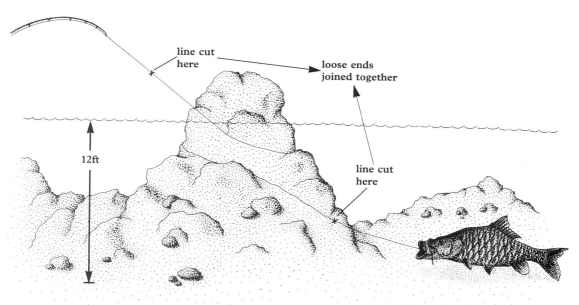

The tethered mahseer.

tie the knot with and I could feel it, kicking against my hand. I reeled the mended line tight, the rod took on its bow and battle was instantly, joltingly resumed.

The fish turned, puts its fins against the current and rattled off a further hundred yards where it stuck again. Once more, dragged over rocks and fallen trees, we followed it to as near the point as possible and again Suban dived. This time, the mahseer had wedged in the dead branches of a monsoon-swept tree. Three times Suban dived into the foam, on each occasion reappearing, eventually, with a piece of dead wood. Through the rod and down the line I could feel what was going on. Gyrations passed up to me as he pulled at the tree or as the fish occasionally thudded its great head. Suban went down a fourth and a last time. Suddenly, the line and fish were both free and Suban pushed the creature away from the snag. Once more we were on the helter-skelter. By now both of us and the fish too were on the surface being carried by the force of the Cauvery towards the lagoon of peace and safety which was ever approaching beneath us. The fish entered first and soon after we followed. Who was the most tired was hard to say, and the mahseer simply wallowed in a deep, still, green water.

'Pump Sir. Pump! Pump!' I was too creased to do anything. 'Pump! Pump, pump!' I stood up, took deep breaths, focused on the fish and pumped. Yard, by precious yard, the fish of my great desire approached the sandbank. Suban stooped, his hand found its mouth and its gills and with a whoop of joy, the impossible was landed.

TONY'S CASSEIN MONSTER

Cassein is known to all carp anglers, not just the travelling ones, as the huge three-armed lake in the south of France that has produced such huge fish and such huge heartache in the past. For many years the water has been a Mecca, but far more people have gone there and failed than have been successful. That is the nature of big waters that are comparatively lightly stocked. But what fish those Cassein carp are! It is hardly surprising that many men have been prepared to put in so much effort for such creatures.

We depart from our usual format for this story from Tony Miles. Most people know of the water and its fish which makes the first two categories superfluous. What Tony goes on to describe is the typical sort of problem that so many people face on this massive water and how he comes to grips with it.

Throughout the book we have tried to avoid the usual glamour story of battles. Here, Tony's stirring account is relevant. A Cassein carp hooked is not a carp on the bank and the battle with these mighty fish in a very deep, snag-strewn water is very much part of the game and should be included. I just love the 'do or die' approach of the battle sequence in this piece. All I can say is that Tony certainly deserved his fish.

A particular fish may come to mind for many reasons. It may simply be the biggest, or the prettiest. It may have taken intense effort to catch, or given the hardest fight. It may have been especially hard to locate or been caught against tremendous odds. It must be extremely rare for one fish to satisfy all these criteria, but that is precisely the case with my personal best carp, a monstrous fish of 58lb from Lake Cassein in the south of France.

Andy Barker and I had arrived in the spring of 1986 to be greeted with far from springlike weather. The previous weeks had been unseasonally cold with heavy rain. Anglers, however, are eternal optimists and, despite receiving the glum news that very few fish were being caught, Andy and I looked round the water on our arrival full of enthusiasm. We even had the encouragement of the first sunny afternoon the region had seen in over a month.

It was slightly discouraging not to have seen evidence of carp after several hours of looking, so we decided to start on one of the gravel bars on the south arm, not far from Chez Pierre. We had ten days at our disposal and by spending the first couple in the vicinity of the restaurant we would be in a good position to glean any information that was available.

That afternoon, exhausted after our long drive, we decided not to fish until first light next morning, after a good sleep. First, however, we prebaited the areas with over two thousand boilies. This prebaiting had a main purpose of attracting the large population of soft crayfish with which Cassein abounds and on which the carp feed heavily. Drawing on my years of chubbing with crays, I knew that there was no better attractor for them than rotten fish and so the boilies for prebaiting were heavily atomized with fish flavourings, far more than for normal baits. The basic baits were Richworth neutrals. Believe me, those baits were rank! We made the mistake of atomizing them in the caravan we had hired for our trip and the van stank of fish for the duration of our stay. Baits for the hairs were three: Tutti Frutti, Salmon Supreme and a trout pellet mixture.

The next morning set the scene for the rest of the trip, in that it was cloudy and cold, with a strong wind. Not long after we had our hookbaits in position the rain started, and it was as well for our peace of mind that we did not know at the time that the rain was to continue unabated for five days, during which the lake was to rise over four feet.

We fished that swim for two days without the slightest hint of a fish. For hour after hour the rain lashed down and with the wind blowing into our pitch it was cold, wet misery. When we packed up on the third morning all our gear was completely drenched and we were in a disconsolate mood. That night, with our gear drying in the caravan, we cheered ourselves up with a civilized meal in Cannes.

The next morning we recommenced operations in a fresh swim further up the south arm, again a purely arbitrary choice as we had not seen a sign of a carp. During the establishing of our camp the rain had been merely a fine drizzle, but that was soon to change. Before all

the rods had been cast out the rain was back with a vengeance, falling with storm force for hour after miserable hour. One by one the Optonics stopped working and it was becoming very depressing. On that day we could actually watch the water rising, a situation that continued steadily until two days later, when we packed up in disgust. Once again everything was awash, and that night in the caravan, with every bit of gear we owned in pieces and drying in front of the fire, including every Optonic, Andy and I plumbed the depths of despair. The trip had taken many months of planning, the anticipation growing to fever pitch at the date of our departure from home. Now here we were, with cold torrential rain hammering on the van roof, almost a week into our trip without a sign of a carp.

That evening we talked for hours. So dispirited had we become that when we got back to the van we were on the brink of cutting our losses and going home early, particularly as the weather forecast gave no promise of a break in the monsoon-like conditions. However, the influence of a few beers and a warm fire raised our spirits and we determined that the next morning we would make one last throw of the dice. Rain or no rain, we would drive around the water in a last attempt to find carp, starting with the west arm, which we had not yet fished. That was to prove a historic decision.

I was awake early that next morning, and the first thing I noticed was the silence, the rain had stopped at last. There was even a patch of blue sky overhead. For several hours that morning we searched the water, much more hopeful of sightings now that the wind had gone. Eventually we stood on a promontory commanding the entrance to a narrow neck between the west arm and the spawning bay. At the same instant we both spotted what for so long we had been searching for. At eighty yards, a tremendous upheaval on the surface was followed by the sight of a huge golden tail, before the carp dived again. That was all we needed to see, and all the old enthusiasm welled back as we unloaded the gear.

A very chunky, foreign fish.

The first thing I did was to get my float rod out. Half an hour of plumbing established the essential features of the swim. We were on the point of a spit of land. Directly in front of us, and to the right, the bay was quite narrow, being perhaps only 70 yards to the opposite, tree-lined bank. To the left it widened out to perhaps 150 yards and here the opposite bank was a steep boulder-strewn cliff. Further left still was the entrance to the bay and the main body of the west arm. Directly in front of us there was a wide gravel bar a uniform 15 feet deep, gradually tailing off to the right to about 22 feet. The fall away to deeper water to the left was steeper, going down to 30 feet fairly quickly. There was a deep channel under the far bank at the narrowest point. All in all, it looked like a perfect place to intercept fish, as they moved in and out of the bay.

As the evening approached carp began rolling regularly and, finally, one of my Optonics burst into life, the first time an alarm had sounded in anger since our arrival a week earlier. Something had picked up three Tutti Frutti boilies on my right-hand rod, presented on the peak of the bar. The line was a blur as it left the spool and as I dropped in the pick up the rod slammed over. Despite being set at almost its tightest drag, the clutch screamed and several yards of line disappeared and Andy reminded me of the snags with which the bed of Cassein is littered. We had already decided to play fish hard, bringing them off the bottom in as quick a time as possible to keep the line

A big fish dives for sanctuary.

free of obstructions. For this reason we were using 18lb Sylcast straight through.

Flipping off the anti-reverse and tightening the stern drag completely, I clamped on the fish, determined that I would only yield line grudgingly by backwinding if I was in imminent danger of being pointed. Holding the fish hard and heaving was the order of the day. Playing the fish on a properly set clutch, as I like to, was a luxury I could not afford. Every foot of line yielded increased the carp's chances of finding a snag and breaking loose.

Ten minutes later, after a really arm-aching scrap, a big carp wallowed in the mesh, and Andy and I gazed at something we had felt we would never see, a 32lb 4oz Cassein carp, the fish that marked the beginning of the end of our nightmare.

It was the following lunch-time when one of my greatest angling moments occurred. Andy and I had just finished photographing my 30-pounder,and one of 26lb with which he had broken his duck, when one of my indicators rose slowly, so slowly that I discounted carp and thought a bream was responsible. I was soon to discover my error, as my strike was the prelude to the most incredible battle I have ever had with a fish. Despite the clutch being set at its tightest, and the reel being clamped in my hand, a fish of unbelievable power tore line off the clutch. For a few seconds I was out of control and the scream from the clutch rose to a high-pitched whine. A huge bow wave headed straight for those boulders on the opposite bank and, knowing that only a few yards separated the fish from disaster, I clamped the rod butt in my groin, clamped the reel face tightly with my hand, and leaned into the fish as hard as I could. The rod was nearly ripped from my hands and it took all my strength to avoid being pointed. I hung on grimly, the rod bending way past its test curve! I could feel the flexing under the reel seat!

For a few seconds all was stalemate and then, with a thunderous roar, an enormous fish surfaced and lashed the water. What an unforgettable sight that was! Foiled in its first attempt to gain sanctuary, the carp now rocketed to my left, heading for more boulders about 150 yards away. The problem now was that I had so much line out that it was impossible to prevent the fish kiting. Applying the heaviest amount of sidestrain possible I only just managed to turn the fish, and with every sinew straining I hauled the carp out of the danger area, gaining a few precious yards in the process. With the fish now swimming towards me for the first time, I crammed on the pressure to keep it in the upper layers of water. About thirty yards out the carp rolled, a huge golden flank and bright yellow tail making me catch my breath. 'Please don't let me lose this' I said aloud.

Andy was a calming influence. 'Just take your time and keep the fish in midwater and he's ours', he said, 'he's well over forty.'

Andy only needed one chance with the net and about twenty minutes after I had first hooked it, a tremendous carp rolled into the landing net. With an almighty heave, Andy hoisted it ashore. Only then did we realize the fish's incredible thickness. Even before we weighed it, Andy reached over and shook my hand. We both knew that this fish was not just big, it was gigantic, but I still could not believe it when Andy declared exactly 58lb. Surely I was dreaming!

Those few moments after the weighing are permanently etched in my memory, a magical moment in time. When I am able to fish no more, I will still see the magnificent proportions of that French leviathan, glinting golden in the warm sunlight. Such memories are beyond price.

PASANG ON THE KARNALI

If we accept that a proper carp challenge means an angler finding a difficult fish in a difficult water and plotting its downfall, often over a long period of time, then a mahseer challenge is hard to find. Most anglers simply cannot afford to spend the amount of time by any Asian river that is necessary if you are to recognize a particular fish and devote time to its capture. Trips are simply too short. Then, of course, there is the problem of identifying particular fish in rivers that are often broad, fast and coloured.

However, there are episodes in the recent history of mahseer fishing that are worth a mention, or more than a mention come to that. For anybody with an angling library, or the desire to build one, I would recommend chapter four of *Somewhere Down the Crazy River* by Paul Boote and Jeremy Wade. This chapter tells of Paul's first and exhausting trip to India where success was chiselled from the face of the sub-continent. It makes compulsive reading and is surely a challenge in its own right. Another book that I would recommend to you is *I Know a Good Place* by Clive Gammon and particularly chapter eighteen called 'The Maharaja Fish'. In that chapter Gammon relates the story of a hugh fish hooked and lost by a young Indian, a fish that he had seen several times before and moved in to catch specifically. Stirring stuff.

Coincidentally, the tale I wish to tell also concerns an Indian, a Nepali guide called Pasang. I met this admirable man and fisherman (it is strange how the two often go together) on a long raft journey down the Bheri River and into the vast Karnali River that flows eventually into the Ganges. It is no secret that this particular journey proved to be a very difficult one for me. Conditions were onerous and the raft itself often quite dangerous; in fact, once I was fairly sure that I had lost my travelling companion, Joy, for ever. However, almost as frustrating was the fact that the mahseer were very hard to capture.

Small clear rivers demand a very cautious approach.

The Bheri and the Karnali are both very fast Himalayan rivers and bait fishing seemed to be an impossibility. Forced back to plugs, the problem was that both rivers ran absolutely crystal clear and every mahseer writer has stressed that this is the kiss of death for angling success. Indeed, I forget the number of times I saw great fish arrow after spoons and spinners in the clear water only to turn away at the last moment. Obviously, my earnest, wooden, plastic and metal creations were seen through completely and treated with suitable derision. Those fish that I did hook – and believe me, there were not many – also tended to come loose after only a couple of minutes' play, indicating they were not hooked at all well in the first place. All in all, it seemed that I was in for a very frustrating trip.

At last, after many days afloat, we decided to settle by the banks of the Karnali where there was a well-organized, comfortable camp that offered a great deal of attractions after the relatively hard living we had been experiencing. The river at this point was magnificent and full of fish, mahseer just as difficult to catch as those we had encountered upstream. Morning after morning, evening after evening, I would trudge back to the camp, hot, irritated, forlorn and fishless. It seemed that there would be no end to my torment as mahseer crept out night-long just beneath our camp.

Enter Pasang. It seemed that he had been watching the river and studying it like any true carp challenge expert. He had found, a mile from the camp, a small feeder stream that wound in from a deep, still lake at the foot of some hills. Believe me, this prospecting on my behalf took some doing: the whole area was

Being a mountain goat helps in the Himalayas!

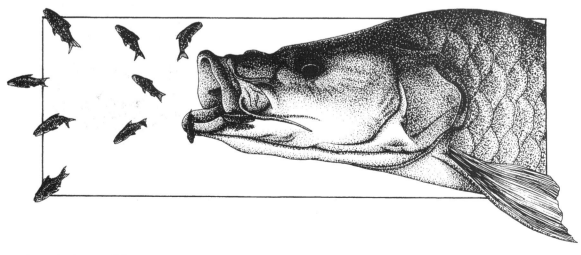

Mahseer chasing small fry.

deep in elephant grass, and known home to at least three tigers.

What Pasang had discovered was that during the night small fish from the lake entered the feeder stream and from there investigated the main river looking for food. The mahseer, as you would expect, had tuned in to this nightly bonus and joined in the fun. The fish were only small, an inch or two long, but their number made for profitable feeding and there the mahseer flocked night after night. An early morning start, Pasang thought, would pay real dividends. There was one more thing: my large spoons and plugs would be useless. I had the choice of either large fly or a very small spinner indeed, the type I had not carried with me. No problem. Out of a small piece of metal and a couple of beads, Pasang constructed an inch-long spoon for me. A Partridge Mahseer Treble completed the business and the next morning, long before the sun rose over the hills, I was following Pasang upstream to the confluence.

We arrived as the light was growing but there was little sign of fish – at first. I began to cast and slowly became aware of odd showers of fish, little pearly things raining out here and there. At first I thought they were evading my spinner but then I saw the case was otherwise – how could I have been so stupid? A wrench on the rod soon showed me that this was real mahseer country and at last I was getting somewhere.

That particular fish weighed 10 or 12lb or so but it did not matter. It was the beginning of a whole run of Nepali fish up to a few pounds over the twenty-mark that I would land during the next handful of dawns and dusks. All night fishing was right out of the question because of the tigers. All in all, I have Pasang to thank for my eventual success on that particular journey. Pasang the Watchful I believe they call him in his village and I can well understand why.

5 STALKING

Not much of an introduction is needed here apart from saying that stalking is far more than a fun way of carping. To many serious carp anglers this aspect of the method has been its undoing for many years; it has seemed that something enjoyable and opportunistic cannot possibly be 'real' fishing. Nothing, in reality, could be further from the truth and now it is common indeed to see a third, stalking rod set up, ready to go, against the side of many bivvies. Opportunism is one thing and it certainly pays to be ready kitted-out to make the most of any chance that comes your way – even at the dead of night something interesting can present itself. However, the majority of the challenges that follow in this chapter are more than mere opportunism; the angler has set out to stalk fish, knowing that this method will often give him the very best opportunity of a serious carp. Above all, it is possible to learn so very much about carp when stalking them. This, if anything, is the real beauty of the method, although many would go for the heart-stopping excitement of seeing a big fish take at close quarters. Whatever, stalking is a real chance for an angler to learn more about his favourite fish and about the best ways to approach them, and that must be good.

THE OPPORTUNIST

Chris Ball has, more than anybody, pioneered the art of using floating baits for carp in Great Britain. It has, of course, long been known that the species will feed avidly on the surface, but Chris has taken the skill to new heights and, even more than that, has publicized the method

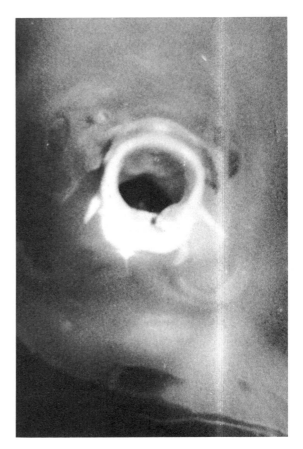

Now there's confidence for you . . .

to a very wide audience indeed. It is often wrongly thought that floater-fishing only works on shallow, easy or well-stocked waters. This is certainly not the case and the challenge Chris describes concerns Savay, long known as one of the most difficult carp waters in Great Britain.

Chris is a busy person and leads the life of a

modern family man and he cannot afford to spend the hours, days, weeks or months even, on hard waters that so many do today. Indeed, on the large, heavily pressured, very difficult carp waters of the Home Counties, we are witnessing the emergence of virtually full-time fishermen. Some of these catch big carp, Chris says, because they are very good anglers and their ability plays an important part. Many, he thinks, catch fish rather because they simply wear them down. As he says, this type of angler keeps on at a swim, at a group of fish until their persistence begins to destroy the carp's defences. The great thing about the approach that Chris describes here is that it is quick, clean and efficient, and large carp were caught without him even forsaking a single night at home in his own bed!

The Water

Savay is one of the most well-known carp waters in Great Britain. It is about seventy acres and beautifully mature, surrounded by tall trees. It is only aesthetically marred by a busy road at the north end of the water and a railway viaduct at the south. Despite the many years of media pressure that Savay has received it can still be quite a lonely water. This is probably because it is very difficult and a most demanding water that pushes carp anglers to their very limits if they are to continue catching.

The Problem

For this challenge we go back to the spring of 1990 when weed began to appear at Savay in

The bay of a pit where floaters may well work.

force. It is important to realize that at this particular time anyway, the vast majority of, if not all, anglers on Savay fished for carp on the bottom. In fact, the water had hardly been attacked at all on the surface. However, as 1990 progressed the weather continued very warm and the weed problem became even greater; as a result, more carp began to come to the top. Neither of these facts meant a great deal to most of the carp fishermen who still continued bottom fishing, sitting outside their bivvies in their swimming trunks, soaking up the sunshine.

The Solution

Chris, as you might expect, did exactly the reverse and went for the carp on the surface. He took with him on his visits to the water a split cane rod and one of the old glassfibre 9ft creations that used to have a leather-bound handle. Albert Romp (still the man who has taken the largest brace of carp at a sitting) asked sarcastically, 'Are we playing golf?' when he saw the little stubby stick that Chris was carrying. 'Albert, I'm going to catch a carp,' was all that Chris retorted.

Typically, observation was the key to Chris's success. Throughout July 1990, north-westerly winds set in, blowing the whole length of Savay down to the end of the canal bank. A long island splits the lake in two and near the bottom of this island lies the Gate Swim, named after the gate situated on the track. Beneath the gate lies the domain of the syndicate members where Chris was not allowed to tread. Remember that he was on a normal season ticket that allowed him to be on the water between six o'clock in the morning and nine at night. Around the Gate Swim, the bank and this Ruislip island converged to a point where they were only forty-five yards apart. Day after day the wind funnelled between these two lengths of bank and the carp became more and more in evidence. In fact, the water was running through this narrow gap more like a river and Chris began to trot baits through.

At first he began to use his cane rod but after losing a fish or two through the very bad weed he moved over to the more meaty fibreglass tool to put maximum pressure on any hooked fish.

Of paramount importance was the feeding. It was imperative to catapult out a dozen pieces of Chum Mixer so that they trotted through the Gate Swim as a tight little group. The hookbait had to be kept as close as possible to them.

The taking area was about twenty yards in length and it took about three to four minutes depending on the strength of the wind for the Chum Mixer biscuits to trot their way through. However, the swirls only came at the end of the trot (the water was moving right to left in front of Chris). There was a large bush hanging out over the swim and this really marked the end of the fishing. However, Chris would let his bait go on for as far as possible, until he could just see it before reeling in. There was also the problem of landing any fish hooked at this extreme range because the bush grew far further out into the water than the short fibreglass rod was long.

Six of seven fish hooked at the extreme part of the swim all went down to the left and fifty per cent became snagged and got away. The rest Chris managed to tease out, often easing the pressure and making them swim back up towards him.

He was observed more than once by Ken Townley in this manoeuvre who simply pronounced him to be a 'stupid idiot!' However, on one of his visits, Ken climbed up a tree and saw some very big fish indeed taking the Chum Mixers. Chris had suspected as much, but Ken's words made him fish even more intensely. He fed the swim very carefully indeed and finally hooked a big fish in front of the bush that turned right and swam up in front of him. However, such was the speed of the fish that it snagged fifty yards away and the hooklength broke.

Composing himself, Chris retackled, checked everything and began to feed again. There were still a few fish present in the swim, taking biscuits in slow swirls that flattened the ripply surface of the lake.

Almost immediately, the hookbait disappeared again in front of the bush and the hooked fish plunged downwards. It was a large, deep fighting carp that finally weighed in at nearly 25lb. A great success indeed for a man fishing odd hours during the daytime on one of the most difficult waters in the country.

As a postscript Chris adds that all the resident carp anglers took note. Before his success the bivvies had all had a third rod, a marker rod, leaning against them. After this particular day, that marker rod almost invariably became a Chum rod! It was shortly after this that Keith Sellick took a 30lb Savay carp on the surface.

FLOATER FISHING EXAMINED

It was Chris Ball as much as anybody else, if not more, who pioneered the new wave of interest in floater-fishing for carp. Obviously the method had never really died from its inception in the 1940s but it did need the boost that Chris gave it. Harry Haskell offers a few more words of valuable advice:

Generally speaking, the margins are the main feature on most waters and, where allowed to do so, carp will frequent them and feed, possibly more than anywhere else. The closer in you fish, especially visual fishing, the more exciting it all becomes. You are more in control, the closer in you fish. Visual carping, be it on the surface or the bottom, is mega-exciting! My early floater experience was à la Walker, crust under the rod top, heart-thumping stuff!

Unfortunately, on many waters, daylight carp keep their distance mostly because of the presence of humans. Thus all sorts of rigs have been devised to get distance, although, of course, the magic of it all decreases in proportion to distance. It is probably true to say that the most popular method is to use a controller and the very successful Chum Mixer –

as long as the carp are still prepared to take it. Chum Mixer has many advantages and although there are numerous alternatives, many have a deficit, in shape, convenience, cost and so on.

At the point of fishing, when using a basic controller and Chum, an observation of mine, and of others for that matter, is that some carpers have a negative approach. The most common shortcomings are putting out too much bait, using crude links, inefficient bait mounting, and, most common of all, casting out too soon.

Carp spend some or many warm daylight hours moving mid-water to a foot or so below the surface, although you will not necessarily see them. Nor do they have to be cruising along with their backs out for floaters to be successful. My suggestions are first, where possible, try to position yourself correctly in relation to the topography of the lake and the prevailing conditions. An ideal place may be on a point with a light wind behind you, or even the opposite. Any strong cross-wind may lead to poor presentation.

A wind lane beloved by the trout will also be a hot taking-spot for carp. Spreading pouchfuls of Mixer all over the place is not generally the productive way to do it. Introduce just two or three close in and let them drift below you for a yard or so, then repeat, and again, until you have established a line of them two or three broad.

The carp will tend to work upwind and you will need sharp eyes for all this, as the first couple to be taken are likely to be very discreetly sipped down. The next one or two may show via a hump in the ripple, this may well be the first you actually notice, although a cast now may prove fatal. Then a mouth appears and down goes another, and again. Cast now, but not at the fish; let it come to you. The idea is to trot your hookbait along at the same pace as the freebies, and this is where experience with other forms of fishing will pay dividends. Trouters and trotters will know what I mean.

Where possible, it is best to watch the Chum,

not the controllers. Carp will and can eject a hookbait just like any other fish. Watch the Chum and for those lips; they can open, close, and open again in a wink. Open, close, strike! In that split second when the mouth closes, your controller will not have moved a jot.

All this is the ideal and within a few rod lengths out. Other situations may well require different techniques. However, successful floater-fishing is all about relative finesse, correct baiting patterns and, above all else, timing.

In flat calm, gin-clear conditions you may clearly see how, from the first intrepid acceptance of the bait, the carp will gain in confidence, stimulating others, and the dream, frenzy feeding. Cast too soon, they go down, leave it too late, or use too many freebies (ten, maybe eight too many) and they have had enough. Timing, timing, timing. Getting it right can be the easiest and certainly the most exciting, of all forms of carping.

Finally, and most importantly, think about your presentation. The diagrams below show one effective method of presenting a Chum and more or less speak for themselves. Floater-fishing at its best is an art form, requiring co-ordination of mind and body, pin-point casting,

and knowing how to use the surface currents and winds and, when stalking individual fish, the hunting instinct. I much admire good floater carpers and their technique is far removed from the beach caster or fixed floater method, left to fish itself at distance, the angler snoozing on the bedchair.

Harry has said it all really and I do not want to labour any points but, in my view, two things do need underlining. First, many people have obviously been attracted to floater-fishing but spent most of their time concentrating on rigs. Harry mentions a couple of good ones and there are several others which are well documented and should prove satisfactory in most conditions. However, and this is the second point, I think that many people have spent too long thinking about rigs and not enough time thinking about and studying the carp itself. Carp are rather like trout when they come to the top and the two forms of fishing, floater-fishing and fly fishing, are not dissimilar. Brian Clarke, in his excellent book *In Pursuit of Stillwater Trout*, first made me aware of the different ways that the trout approaches the dryfly in particular or an emerging nymph. The vary-

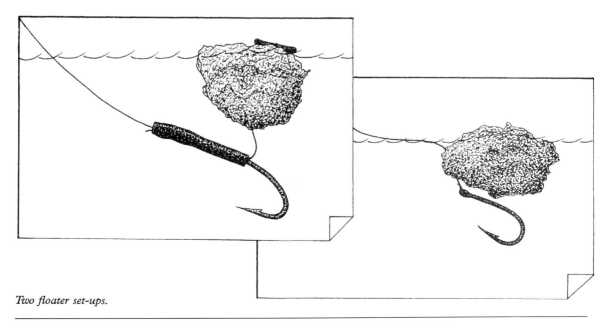

Two floater set-ups.

That carping maestro with a 20lb fish in 1969.

ing takes indicate different moods on the trout's part and the successful fly-fisherman learns to recognize this piscatorial body language.

As Harry says, the confident surface-feeding carp is easily spotted: it approaches baits in an easy, gentle fashion with its head showing and a great deal of its shoulders. The surface baits are slurped down slowly and without any real commotion whatsoever. The whole process is

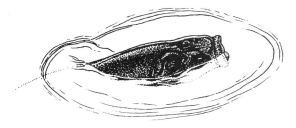

Carp taking a floater confidently.

as placid as a cow grazing on the home meadow. More wary carp approach floating baits in totally different ways, often snatching at bait or exploding on the surface. Often they will come out of nowhere and just take one bait before disappearing again and sometimes they will gobble three or four baits and then leave the area altogether. These fish are virtually uncatchable from the top and the greatest effort should be put into thinking about feeding patterns and how to lull the fish into total confidence. Then, to an extent, whatever your rig the fish will be catchable. That is the challenge.

RICHARD'S SOLUTION

Richard Slater is a young man for whom I have a great deal of respect. He came to see me some years ago, when just eighteen, with a view to journeying to the Ganges to catch a mahseer – a brave thing to undertake as a young man with no experience of Asia. I gave him every bit of information that I could and Richard acted on it and added to it; the result was a splendid Indian mahseer. Everything that Richard does regarding his fishing – and carp are his passion – is undertaken with the same energy, enthusiasm and logic – the hallmark of this challenge.

The Water

The pit is a flooded clay-working of about two-and-a-half acres, quite old, divided distinctly into two areas. There are the shallows that are between five and six feet deep, riddled with islands and bars, and there is the deeper water, about an acre and a half of it, where depths approach fourteen or fifteen feet. In the shallows, throughout the summer, the weed grows literally from top to bottom and that is where the carp spend virtually all their time, generally nights included. The water is very rich, in the shallows especially, and the carp spend a great deal of time simply rolling there, fins out, enjoying the bountiful gifts of life! You can,

Ashlea Pool: the tiny water where stalking really took off as an acknowledged method.

Richard says, pepper the fish with Chum Mixers and other floaters for a long time without any response whatsoever. Fish simply have no need of artificial baits.

The Fish Stocks

Originally the pit held roach, rudd and a head of big tench, but about eight years ago thirty to forty carp were stocked and have grown well indeed. Today there are very few under 10lb and the average weight is about sixteen, with at least one known fish into the low to mid twenties. The carp are obviously growing fast in what is a rich, Midland pit.

The Problem

Simply, in 1992, the carp were just not picking up baits at all. They tended to avoid the deep water where bottom baits could be fished in conventional fashion and in the weed they were not interested in anything whatsoever. One of Richard's colleagues spent a whole day fishing floaters all around the pit and only managed to hook one single fish – and that was the result from a very experienced floater fisherman on an ideal floater day. So, fish quite content with the natural stocks of food, reluctant to come to the top and hardly ever picking up a bottom bait – a challenge indeed.

The Solution

Richard realized that he would have to find fish showing some sort of movement and then present something that they wanted very accurately to them. In the end, after a great deal of observation and foraging, he found the site of an old feeder stream entering the top end of the lake, where the shallows met thick undergrowth. It was not easy to get Richard's 6ft 4in in there, but he managed it and in a slight depression, mercifully free of weed, he saw some carp moving quite freely for a short while.

He stayed there most of the day, watching, and found that the fish visited the area every hour or so. The next day he reappeared with a can of sweetcorn and put a couple of handfuls in the depression created by the old feeder stream. The carp, on cue, came from the thick weed into his baited area. Soon their tails were in the air and the water muddied. He did not need any further prompting.

His rod was an 11ft, 2lb test curve home-built affair with 12lb main line, while 6in of multistrand on a size six hook completed the entire rig – one that had to be very sound to keep fish away from the forest of snags and logs that surrounded his area.

More corn went in and as soon as the fish began to appear the second time he simply lobbed 10ft of line out and the bait settled, along with the free offerings. In short, one fish was lost and four fish between 16lb 10oz and 12lb 8oz were landed.

These carp were not hard to catch once their movements had been deciphered. Again, the key word was sanctuary, and this short tale describes true stalking in every sense of the word. That one day saw Richard's tally of carp for the whole season so far doubled!

MICK'S SEVENTEEN

There are some excellent characters in this sport of ours and Mick Brown wrote to me from a hospital bed.

Please forgive the scrawl. It is one o'clock in the morning and I am lying on my back in the Edith Cavell Hospital. I am in excruciating pain and it is 16 June, the first opening day that I have missed since 1963! You will appreciate, John, that the last thing on my mind is fishing! I cannot get to the phone but will give this rather untidy letter to my sister to post.

I have caught dozens of carp of 20lb or more on bolt-rigs but I do not feel any achievement in their capture. The ones that I count as special are those that I have stalked – real one-to-one battles. Indeed, my carp fishing seems to have gone round in a full circle just lately. When I started my carp fishing I used stalking tactics and although I have gone through all the different stages of carp fishing I find that this most basic of approaches gives me more satisfaction than any other. I am not saying that it catches more or bigger fish, but to equate statistics with pleasure is a sure recipe for frustration. More and more, my summers are spent roaming around with just one rod and less time is spent sitting behind rods and waiting. I have always been a fidgety sort of angler, always wondering if there are any fish moving in the next swim or even at the other side of the lake. For me, sitting still and not catching for just a couple of hours is a real trial of endurance.

We all need to decide what matters most in our fishing and not be influenced by what others say about what we do. We need to decide whether the results justify the means. Is it worth sitting in a swim for a whole week for a couple of fish? Many obviously do think so and good luck to them. You need to ask yourself, though, if you are fishing for the right reasons. Is it for the sport or the result? My mind is made up on that one and, for me, a seventeen-pounder hooked close to the bank that strips fifty yards of line off the reel is far more exciting than winching in a much bigger fish through a reed-bed on heavy tackle. To hook a big fighting fish close-in by stalking is for me the ultimate achievement.

So, what does stalking entail? Basically, it is casting a bait to a fish you know is there

Stalking generally demands a more cautious approach than this! Carp maestri Yates, James and Miller study the water.

advantages but, as often as not, I prefer a 12ft rod which enables me to reach further to lower baits on to fish I have spotted or perhaps stand a little further back from the bank if they are close-in. The important thing is that the tackle must take the explosive rush of speed as you put the hook in. Even a modest ten-pounder will go off like an express train and your tackle will be well tested, believe me! Hooked at this range, they are like different animals compared to those hooked at eighty yards towing big leads behind them.

I prefer to fish as light as conditions will allow me to, or at least within reason. Ideally, I like to use a 1¼lb test curve rod with 6lb or 8lb line. The nature of many summer swims and the size of the fish I am after, however, often sees me using a 2¼lb test curve rod and

because you can either see it or because it is giving itself away by making some disturbance. The fish need not necessarily be close-in either, as fish can be spotted quite some way out and cast to with surface baits.

By its very nature, stalking involves creeping up on unsuspecting fish and obviously the quieter the banks are the better. This eliminates some waters completely and it is only feasible on others at certain times, notably mid-week, early morning or in the dark.

One of the things that I like about stalking is that the tackle required is minimal and it is ideal for the opportunist or short-session man like myself. You do not need to own a bivvy, rod pod or Optonics to call yourself a carp angler. That is only one aspect of it. This sort of carping can be done with the bare essentials. Under trees and bushes a short rod has its

Even moderate carp from lilypads can test tackle to the limit.

Definitely not the stalking approach!

12lb line. Do not think that you can get away with underfilled spools either, just because you are fishing close-in. A good fish, out of control, can easily strip seventy or eighty yards off the reel.

Anyway, let us move on to the capture I want to talk about.

The Water

The water is a sixty-acre gravel pit in Lincolnshire with gin-clear water and a very few, difficult-to-catch carp. Because of this, it tends not to be very heavily fished.

The Problem

A small group of carp had taken up semi-permanent residence in a very thick reed-bed.

They could be seen in the gaps next to the bank, but to hook one would mean a certain loss as the reeds extended about twenty feet from the bank. They would surely bolt through this reed fringe towards open water and get caught in the thick wall. I would never risk hooking fish that might get damaged or tethered in the reeds and for a long time I had to dismiss these fish as 'no-hopers'.

The Solution

One morning, when the fish had moved out into the open water, I put on my shorts and pumps and waded into the reed-bed with a cutting tool at the end of a landing-net stick. The water was chest deep and the bottom was surprisingly contoured with deep holes and with seemingly bottomless silt. The idea was to

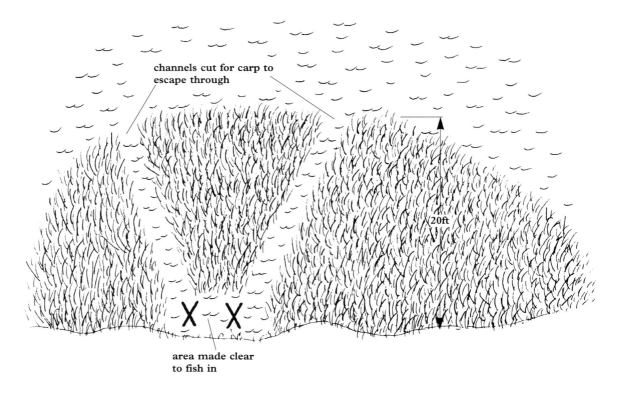

channels cut for carp to
escape through

20ft

area made clear
to fish in

Mick's seventeen.

cut escape routes for the carp. The plan was that they would get used to reaching the open water beyond via the channels that I was cutting. I took out anything that looked like it would damage the line if a fish bolted past it. A few snags were also removed and the gaps were tidied up and made perfect.

A few days later I returned and on an idyllic summer morning I came across a small group of fish browsing on the silt and weed stems. Two small slugs were soon obtained from a nearby ditch for bait, threaded on to a size four hook and lowered gently to the confidently feeding carp. With no delay, one turned on to its side and sucked in the tasty titbit.

I pulled the hook home and, exactly according to plan, a bow-wave powered through one of the prepared channels and away from any danger of snagging. I was able to play the fish

out in open water and ten minutes later the virgin 17lb fish begrudgingly inched over the drawstring. Forget pounds and ounces, this is fishing!

A NOTE ON RICH WATERS

It might be of interest here, after having looked at one of these particularly rich natural waters, to quote from two letters that I recently received. The first one came from Mr Biggs of Surrey who wrote:

I must apologize for intruding on your privacy by writing this letter. However, I know of no other way of finding out something that has puzzled me for a very long time.

You have often stated that fish, in particular

cyprinids, lie around during mid-summer and partake of food in the form of soup – that is they are sucking in and retaining the various forms of zooplankton from the microscopic up to daphnia.

I have watched fish at numerous times apparently sucking in this soup. However, I have great difficulty in coming to terms with the fact that they are retaining it for consumption. Surely carp are not equipped with filter hairs with which to sieve out the water taken in, such as a whale has. Any water sucked in is dispelled via the gills and as far as I know does not pass through the gut or at least a major part of it.

For guidance I contacted Dr Bill Barber, a fish-farmer in Scotland with a PhD in coarse fish and their feeding characteristics. His reply was interesting.

I have an incomplete knowledge of carp but I do know from my own knowledge of roach (a fellow cyprinid) that even large, mature specimens do not just browse on species of *Daphnia* (*Daphnia* as a generic name should always be written in this way). Rather they feed selectively on the largest 'bits of the soup'. When they eat *Daphnia*, although cyprinids they are equipped with pharyngeal teeth, the hard exoskeletons of *Daphnia* and relations are not destroyed so that I can compare the size distribution of *Daphnia* found in the gut with that collected from the water at the same time. Since there was a distinct possibility of the *Daphnia* not being evenly distributed in the lake (that is the fish grazing in an area favoured by the large *Daphnia*) I followed this up with laboratory experiments. I presented fish in tanks with *Daphnia* of known size, distribution and number at regular intervals to see how the size and distribution of the *Daphnia* in the tank changed. I was also getting some idea of the fish's potential feeding rate.

These combined observations showed that roach have a considerable ability to browse on *Daphnia*. In my PhD thesis I listed eighteen pages that demonstrated this effect for other species including carp. As you probably know,

the char, in the absence of fish cages providing a rain of unnatural food, feed on minute organisms. There is no specialized equipment in char either and they just repeatedly see, pick and eat pieces of zooplankton that appeal.

The conclusions are that many fish feed on zooplankton but do not have gill-rakers. Gill-rakered fish swim around with their mouths open and strain the water. Roach and carp pick and eat individual items. One of my experiments showed that a roach can pick and eat over one hundred individuals each minute. Finally, I found that roach, and presumably carp also, switched to a *Daphnia* diet only when *Daphnia* became exceptionally abundant in the lake – a classic opportunistic feeding syndrome.

It would seem, then, that carp will become preoccupied with larger *Daphnia* when they exist in the water in a great enough quantity. It could well be that at these times boilies do not seem at all an attractive bait. Of course, I am referring here to still, small waters; estate lakes are the recurring example and I freely admit that boilies have their rightful place on larger, cooler waters like gravel pits.

THE SINGLE-HANDED APPROACH

Dave Davies is a man I feel very fortunate to have met and to have fished with. He has an intuitive approach to waters, somehow blending in with them until they become a part of each other and understanding is total. This is a gift that Dave shows particularly well, I feel, in this exacting challenge.

The Water

The pit is roughly triangular, and surrounded for the most part by tall trees. The most heavily wooded bank has been left untouched, partly to allow wildlife to flourish, and partly because of the boggy nature of the bank. Unfortunately, from my point of view, this is the shallow bank. The water is no deeper than three feet along this bank; the shallows being about twenty yards wide before shelving away fairly sharply into six to eight feet of water. There is also quite heavy weed growth along this stretch; in the remainder of the pit there are sporadic clumps of sub-surface weed.

The swim from which I fished the early part of the season enabled me to cast two rods across the shallows (about seventy or eighty yards) and put a third bait next to a large weed clump about twenty yards from my bank in five feet of water.

The Problem

I have fished for carp periodically for twenty years or so, but do not qualify for the title carp angler as I have too much interest in other fish to be able to concentrate solely on one species. My winters are spent pike fishing, I like the odd summer session for bream and tench, and I am currently having a lot of fun after river roach with an 11m pole.

However, my quarry during the summer is mainly carp, and I have spent the past few seasons at a hugely prolific local gravel pit, well known for its massive head of high quality commons. All species of fish in the pit grow to a decent size. Couple this to the fact that club membership is quite large and you will appreciate that the water is inevitably crowded during the summer. Whilst I enjoy good fishing, I dislike excessive company!

So, last season I decided to consider my options, and the best sounded like the question in Rod Hutchinson's catalogue, 'X is a pit reputed to hold a few decent carp which have never been fished for. How would you approach it?' This is an account of my approach.

The water in question lies about twenty-five miles from my house and is an established gravel pit of about three acres. It has an extremely restricted membership and I have fished there for three years, mainly during the

winter for pike. All of the other members fish purely for enjoyment, happy to take whatever comes along. During the close-season, I decided to try to establish roughly how many carp the pit contained. Information from other members suggested between three and fifty, with the majority saying fewer than ten. No one I spoke to had caught a carp, but a fish of 12lb or so had apparently been landed a few years previously. I myself had only ever seen one carp, a common which leapt out of the water one winter's day, while I had the pike rods out.

With this information, I had then to decide if the project was feasible. In its favour was the fact that I would be fishing for uncaught fish with no competition. On the other hand, I had to recognize that there was only a handful of fish whose habits I knew nothing about. My time was also limited mainly to weekends and further limited by the fact that, as captain of a village cricket team, I could not miss too many Sundays. Despite what would inevitably be a single-handed approach, I figured that a number of relatively short sessions coupled with the odd overnight stay, should enable me to learn something about the fish. I also had the advantage of being able to fall back on the prolific water and catch a fish or two when the need arose. My mind was made up, now I had to consider my approach.

The Solution

Bait was originally a difficult decision for me; these fish were uncaught and would probably take any well-presented bait. Nonetheless, I decided to stick to a boilie which had been successful for me over the past two years, both at the aforementioned pit and also on the occasional visit to another small water. The base was SBS 100 mix, and I had learned to make a batch of 26oz (0.74kg) of the bait to six size 2 eggs. I found this simpler than trying to match sufficient eggs to 1lb (500g) of bait. Attractors took the form of 7½ml SBS Kiwi Fruit, 6 drops of Spearmint Essential Oil and

20ml Aquamino. I felt that my circumstances demanded an attractor bait, and this one had worked before.

My original thinking on presentation was again on the lines that virgin fish would need no special end tackle arrangements, and consequently I began with Ultima nylon hooklengths, and ordinary bottom-fished baits. Before long, I realized the senselessness of this and changed to Silkworm hooklengths and buoyant baits. It is quite likely that the carp would have taken ordinary baits on nylon hooklengths, but having chosen a bait that had worked before, I needed for consistency's sake to fish it in the same manner. For similar reasons, I used running leads; I wanted to know if anything occurred at the business end.

I spent quite a few hours at the pit during the close-season, during which time I had seen fish only once, a dark shape pushing through the far bank weed. I felt that the weather had been sufficiently conducive to fish-spotting to confirm the view that very few fish indeed were present, and with this in mind I turned to thoughts of prebaiting. I understand that pre-baiting with non HNV baits will not produce any kind of recognition in food value terms from fish. On the other hand, I felt it would be useful to get the fish to understand that this bait was food. As a result, I introduced bait about twice a week for five or six weeks before the season opened, putting in about 150 small baits on each occasion.

For the first few weeks of the season, I fished from the swim mentioned earlier, mostly sessions of nine or ten hours from dawn to midday, or midday to dusk, and I also managed the odd overnight stay. The near swim would be fed with hemp seed, and fished with pop-up in conjunction with a dozen or so free offerings. I have always found hemp to be a great attractor, but I discovered on this occasion that a shoal of 4lb bream was in residence in this area. The longer rods were fished with buoyant or pop-up bait, with a scattering of eighty or ninety free offerings in the general area. Incidentally, I always use a grass stalk or something

similar as a hair stop and I have taken to pinching a small shot immediately behind the bait to hold it firmly in place. Neutral buoyancy baits sit very neatly like this.

During July and August the very warm weather created changed conditions in the pit. The water level fell between two to three feet, the water became slightly coloured and much of the weed growth died off. Of most relevance to me was the fact that the far bank shallows became dry land. I felt that this would act in my favour, as the area where my baits were going now became the natural margin for patrolling fish.

Late in August, an evening session produced two good tench, the first from the pit on boilies. I am always undecided about this kind of event, but take comfort from the fact that the bait must be attractive, if only to the 'wrong' fish. Early in September, a run of northerly winds set in; these blew across the shallows and on a couple of occasions I fished hopeful of action.

On 9 September I arrived at eleven o'clock in the morning for the session planned to last until about nine in the evening. I found my friend Phil fishing my chosen swim, catching livebait for the forthcoming pike season. Phil was on the verge of packing up and, not for the first time that year, wished me luck.

The weather was unusual. A north-westerly was pushing steadily on to the shallows, but the day felt warm, with overcast skies. I had long ago abandoned the close-in rod, and now fished two rods across. Both baits were popped-up, but as a change from normal procedure one bait was orange, to stand out from all other red baits. At noon I was installed and fishing.

By five o'clock my tackle was packed away. Two significant events had occurred. At half past three I had landed a mirror carp of 20lb 14oz. At a quarter past four I had landed a mirror carp of 26lb 12oz. I was speechless.

The first fish had taken the red bait, and after initial struggles had come to the net fairly smoothly. The capture of this fish gave me enormous pleasure, and I relaxed on my chair in a euphoric state arranging a fresh bait.

Having done this, I cast it straight up into a tree above me! As it was an alder I had to break the line. With a fish captured, I could not raise the necessary enthusiasm to retackle. Instead, I fished on with one rod moving the bait to the same spot that produced the fish.

I was aghast at the second take. I could only believe that it was the same fish again, particularly as there was no real fight, beyond dour resistance. On the surface it was obviously a different fish and parting the net mesh revealed a hug pot-bellied lump. Not the prettiest fish in the world, but then, I am not the prettiest angler!

I did not dare cast out again for fear that the spell might be broken.

The memory of that brilliant afternoon will last a long time, but it is not too distant for me to take stock of my approach. First and foremost, I had tried to reduce the number of variables; bait and tackle were those that had worked before. Secondly, I had not placed too much reliance on the estimates of other people as to the numbers of fish, and felt that it paid to underestimate their numbers when it came to baiting up. Thirdly, I had benefited from the advantage of the 'fall-back' water, somewhere to get a bend in the rod and a fish in the net, which I have always found a great stimulus in these sort of circumstances. Fourthly, I had been prepared not to catch, in fact, I half expected not to – a mental preparation that is necessary for a single-handed approach.

THE WELL KNOWN TALE OF ERIC

The Water

The Railway Lake is about four acres in extent with a maximum depth of about fifteen feet and an average depth of between five and seven feet. It is generally clear but sometimes clouds. It is moderately rich, although now quite an old pit, and holds a comparatively low head of carp, although more were introduced in the early 1980s. It is surrounded by trees and the extensive lily beds are a feature. The water is now privately owned but was once a jewel in the crown of the local authority, attracting a host of very capable anglers.

The Fish

Eric was certainly the target fish for many years and for many anglers. There were, by the end, about eight or nine other decent fish up to perhaps eighteen pounds before forty or so smaller fish were introduced. There was also the very occasional big bream (down to one at the end) with tench and roach and a few rudd. Eric (a strange name, as it turned out, for a fish found dead, apparently unable to pass her eggs) was probably the longest lived of a stocking that took place in the early 1950s. Ken Smith, a Norfolk fish farmer and matchman of fame, with two or three friends took a bucket of small carp and scattered them here and there throughout East Anglian pits and ponds. This haphazard stocking was a great success and provided the bed-rock of big fish from the mid–1960s until the mid–1980s when Eric finally died. He was found, badly set up and is now being repaired. He is to be seen at the Ratcatchers Inn, near Booton, Norwich.

In life, in his prime, Eric was a leather, with a distinctive peach-gold belly. He was caught at least twice, both times weighing in the low thirties. Possibly at his peak, he just climbed to 34 or 35lb but we cannot know that for sure.

I said Eric was probably the last of that stocking. There have been many rumours of a far bigger common which I believe I saw last in 1985. That is, I know I saw it but as no one ever caught it I would not want to hazard a guess as it its weight. It was, however, massive and a good example of how a monster can hide in even the smallest of waters.

The Problem

Many years of angling pressure had made Eric very cautious of tackle and baits as they existed

One of Eric's lesser companions takes a piece of floating crust, something Eric probably had not done for the last ten years of his life.

in the mid–1980s. He had seen and dealt with most varieties of both and in the last years of his life he seemed to be less likely than ever to make mistakes. The introduction of thirty to forty smaller carp made no real difference to him and he did not seem to be concerned in the face of more competition. All the introduction of small fish did was make it much harder to leave a bait in place for any amount of time.

Through the summers of 1984 and 1985 I found it impossible to prebait without keeping the ravenous immigrants at bay. Each time a smaller fish was captured, Eric was simply warned off that particular bait or pitch.

There was some hope in that when Eric fed, he often really blitzed into a carpet of baits.

This did not happen often, however, and these gluts were of short duration. Also, as Eric used the entire pool it was very hard, if not impossible, to predict his movements.

A Solution

However, at times Eric was given to feeding just as hard on surface baits and this appeared to be a definite chink in his armour, especially as he could be seen at the top and a bait could be withdrawn from an intruding nuisance fish. Another bonus was that his surface feeding generally took place at dusk, very often under a particular canopy of branches.

Since the lake had become private, I was unaware of anyone trying hard on the surface

Nearly Eric's downfall. . . though remember she was a leather!

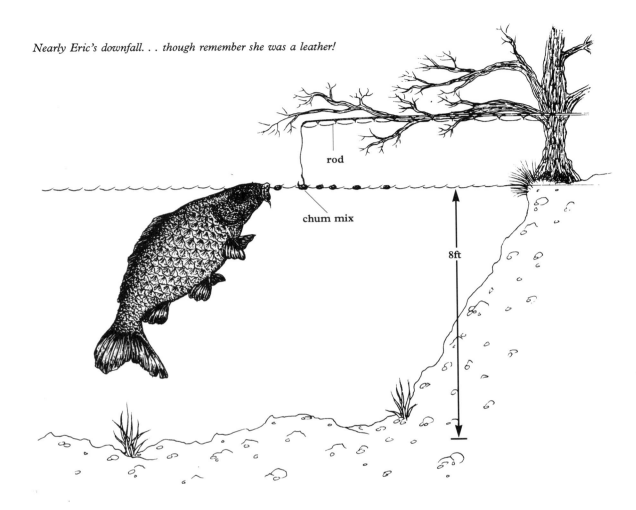

rod

chum mix

8ft

and felt it very likely that Eric had not seen dog biscuits before as, believe it or not, they were relatively new at that particular time as a mainstream bait. The plan could not have been more simple: I would simply arrive at the Railway Lake in the late afternoon, watch for Eric and, as the sun set, begin to feed a suitable, tree-shaded area. Nor was I going to take any chances with the presentation: my plan was to use a 17ft rod built for me by John Wilson in the days when we were missing hundreds of bream bites a night. The idea was that this barge-pole would sweep yards more line through the water than the standard 11ft or 12ft foot rod. Since alternative answers to

bream bites had been found, the rod had lain idle until it was now resurrected. The plan was simply to use its length to push through the alders and dap a biscuit on the surface without any line showing on the water whatsoever. I could present a bait four yards from the bank like this and the rod would not be seen against the foliage. The choice of this rod was to prove critical.

On the fourth night Eric simply tore into the biscuits I had introduced. He was approaching from the left, moving to the right and gobbling everything that had drifted into the open water. He must have taken a dozen when all went quiet. Two minutes later he was at my feet, his nobbled head pushing out of the water and biscuits disappearing rapidly. He began to move out from the bank underneath the alder branch, feeding with absolute confidence. All I had to do was lower a biscuit; he would be at the exact spot within a minute.

I froze. So close, in the gloom, Eric looked huge and formidable. I panicked about the rod. It had never caught a single fish and now, with the challenge so close to a climax, I lost faith in my tools. Whilst I dithered there in the dark, Eric ate all before him and passed out again into the open water. He mopped up the last, stray biscuit and disappeared.

I was not too worried and, stupidly, even congratulated myself on my decision. The next night I returned with a proven carp rod and, sticking to the same plan, I prepared to fish a bait six to eight feet out. I did not get a chance

– not then, not ever. I had squandered my opportunity. Mentally I was up to the challenge but my courage had deserted me. I know now that I would have put a hook into Eric that night and I like to think that I have never been found wanting in a similar situation since.

As a postscript, I tried that 17ft rod later on pike and other carp. It would have pulled a barn down, let alone land a 30lb leather!

ATTENTION TO DETAIL

The history of the hunt for Eric is an interesting one and underlines the importance of minute attention to detail in any testing challenge, especially when the fish is of the age and intelligence that this great leather had managed to achieve. Attention to detail can really be

Eric's home today.

the key – an absolutely vital one – and not the slightest thing can be left to chance. Just how you intend to present the hookbait is critical. Harry Haskell talks us through the considerations.

I have been asked, on numerous occasions, if it is worth going to all this trouble, whipping hairs, colour blending link material hooks and leads and soap.

Whipped hairs are a personal preference of mine for the majority, but not all, of the time when I use a hair. Today, there are several types of clear or coloured silicon tubing available, which are both practical and discreet in use, and I would doubt that any advantage is gained from using whipped hairs on large hooks and baits in some situations. But then again, there are no disadvantages either.

Carp's ejection or rejection of food or other substances by blowing out is well documented. Therefore, in line with this thinking, it can be assumed that ideally the hookbait, upon ejection, needs to be somewhere below the hook-eye, thus helping to prick the fish. For this to happen will depend upon the hook type and size, the hair length and position tied upon the hook itself. It is theoretically possible to arrange for the hook and bait to go into and out of the mouth together, or either one leading or lagging each other. However, a hair which comes away from the top of the hook-shank, approximately in line with the hook-point, has been proved to be an acceptable and successful compromise.

This compromise can only be regarded as a starting point though. The need for adjustments is indicated, as usual, by lack of action, but only when you think a more positive response should have materialized. These adjustments may be made by increasing or decreasing the hook size and/or hair length in relation to the hookbait diameter.

I subscribed to the view that the hook size should proportionally always be in balance with the bait and this seems to be generally good thinking. However, there have been times when a proportionally unbalanced relationship has been successful, for example a size ten to an 18mm boilie or a size four with a 10mm boilie or single particle. Generally, I find the use of small hooks (eight or ten) and baits more productive where it is possible to use them and I worry about the gape of standard twelves and smaller, so rarely use them for sizeable carp. The popular size six is reserved for larger baits and/or tough situations, and I have recently rarely used fours. Mind you, back in the 'spud-and-crust' days size $\frac{1}{2}$/0s were often successfully employed. The choice of size requires other considerations apart from its relationship with bait diameter, and the material it is tied to is one of them.

As mentioned earlier, there are no disadvantages in giving prior thought and effort to how you intend to present the hookbait. The same applies to colour blending leads and choosing complementary link material. I will admit that colour blending swivels and hooks may possibly be going too far at times. However, the philosophy I endeavour to follow at the hook end and back as far as possible, is all about attention to detail and neatness of presentation. I am convinced that the value of the whole is greater than the sum of the individual parts.

Meaningful and consistent practical evidence to support this philosophy is not too difficult to find and indeed experience for yourself. For example, when two carpers fish the same swim with the same baits, I would bet on the angler who adopts my recommended philosophy to consistently have more pick-ups.

If you can accept this, we may then agree that there are some situations where finesse does not matter too much and times when it does. The point is this: those times when it matters will not necessarily be known to you at the point of fishing – indeed, the only indication you may have is no indication. Therefore assume that it always matters, even if at times it does not. For the expenditure of a little effort on your part, you have nothing to lose and a lot to gain by adopting this thinking.

An advanced carper knows there is always a

reason for lack of action; there are no exceptions to this rule. It is down to you to seek out the reason and, through options, take action. The search can start, for example, by re-evaluating the type of water being fished and, even more specifically, that area in front of you. Despite the wide diversity of carp waters and the carp therein throughout Great Britain, they can be categorized and the following generalizations spring to mind. From this list I would expect to need to apply more attention to detail and finesse of presentation for situations deriving from the left-hand side than the right.

No doubt some will be on their backs, legs in the air, after viewing this! Nonetheless, remember that we are talking about the value of offering finesse, colour blending links and leads, pinning down links and lines behind leads and so on, and not debating easy and hard waters, otherwise too many contradictions are evident.

For instance, all soft-bottomed waters are generally far more problematic in terms of presentation than hard-bottomed waters. This is simply because it is physically much easier for you to get the presentation 'right' when fishing over a firm bed, including hard spots, in an otherwise silty lake. Once this presentation and bait is offered over any clear, clean, firm area, it is much more exposed and it is this very exposure which leaves your effort open to detailed inspection. Paradoxically, that which is easier for you to achieve may well prove unacceptable for the carp, although this may become acceptable with time.

The identical presentation placed under bushes, in debris, weed, reeds, lilies, in either firm or soft-bottomed waters, is not exposed to the same extent by blending in with and becoming part of all those twigs, dead leaves and reed stalks. If you can physically get it right, a bait in such places is sometimes picked up very quickly. Thus the composition of that small area of the lake-bed where your presentation is offered can be fundamentally important, and how many times do you know specifically what this composition is? At best, it is often no more than an educated guess.

To summarize, I would suggest that the more exposed our presentation is, the more important it is to pay attention to detail. It is my experience that endeavouring to offer perfect presentation in easy waters will double the average pick-up rate and on harder waters that pickup will hopefully happen within a more acceptable time-scale. All things being equal of course, a phrase which duly lets me off the hook!

AND ALL THE REST

Carp fishing is an absurdly narrow title to give to the vast spectrum of sport it encompasses. The richness of carp fishing is little challenged by any other type of angling, possibly with the exception of trout fishing which has virtually as many opportunities. A carp angler can fish for great, barrelled gravel-pit carp, for crucians or for wildies. Carp are fished for by specialists, by pleasure anglers and increasingly by matchmen. There are, in most waters, big carp and moderate carp and there are also hard carp and easy carp. There are carp in Great Britain and also in most other places in the world. You can fish for carp on the top or on the bottom. You can pursue carp winter and summer. In fact, there is always something new and different to be done somewhere in the world of carp, and perhaps these challenges reflect that.

WILD CARDS

The Fish and the Waters

As far as I am aware, all the populations of wild carp that I will talk about here originated from Saham Toney Mere in central Norfolk. This is a very large, circular reeded water, reputedly of very great age, that during the mid–1900s held extensive stocks of almost certainly genuine wild carp. During the late 1950s and to my certain knowledge the mid–1960s, many of these fish were distributed to a clutch of waters in North Norfolk. In many cases the stockings did very well and the older fish survived for many years – and are probably still living today – and in some cases spawned suc-

cessfully. This means that we are talking about groups of wild carp of great age and experience.

The fish were moved into many waters, but a few presented extreme problems. One is a very small, circular farm pond of perhaps three-quarters of an acre. The second is an ancient duck flight, very shallow and possibly reaching an acre in extent. The third water is a fifteenth-century moat and the fourth water, the smallest of them all, is a marl pit that I doubt covers a third of an acre but does have quite deep pockets up to eleven or twelve feet. All these waters present their own, different challenges.

Problems and Solutions

Over-Fishing

The circular farm pond became known as a wildie water of prominence in the late 1960s and for the next twenty years was put under considerable pressure by many local anglers, both old and young, experienced and novice. The carp in the water were caught again and again and began to show remarkable awareness of traditional baits and methods. Soon, too, they began to become wary of boiled baits, particles, hair-rigs, bolt-rigs and everything that man's ingenuity could dream up.

Fish were, of course, still caught, but at ever more infrequent intervals; most infuriating was the fact that one very large wild carp indeed had been caught twice in the 1970s at about 10lb. That particular fish became a target to many of us who fished there. By the early 1980s, after the fish had not been seen for many years, doubts arose as to whether it was still alive. After all, the water was tiny and very

A wildie or a common? Probably the latter judging by the depth and solidarity of the frame.

shallow and surely the fish would have to have fallen sooner or later to someone.

It was then, in some desperation, that an acquaintance of mine decided to ignore the carp altogether and fish for the eels – rumour had it that some real leviathans were present. Accordingly, his visits to the lake now saw him legering with small deadbaits. You have guessed it! On his third trip, legering half a small dace, he hooked, played and lost at the net a wild carp that he estimated to be almost a yard long. There could be little doubt that this was the extraordinary fish that we had all wanted to see for so long and it was bad luck that it was lost at the very last moment.

That, however, did not matter particularly; a total change of baits – something none of us would have thought of using – had done the trick. Also, of course, proof was now there for us all that the great fish had lived, unscathed, through so many years of high angling pressure.

Shallow Water

Things are not quite as bad at the old duck flight now. In 1991 the water had become shallow to the point of extinction but fortunately the landowner acted promptly and had it dug out once again to its original depth of some two or three feet. However, in the late 1980s the water was only about four to six inches deep, barely enough to cover the backs of the seventy or so fish that lived in the lake. Hard winters were not much of a problem as they simply disappeared into the mud, but from spring onwards the shoals could easily be seen, backs and tails out of the water as they foraged.

The problem was a simple one: the water was so shallow that the fish were aware of everything around the bankside. In fact, their eyes were often clear of the water itself and there is no doubt that they could see any angler approach. It was easy enough to spot a wildie shoal moving around, but stalking it seemed to be virtually impossible. As soon as you approached within ten yards or so, the fish simply panicked and scattered.

One partial solution was to cast to the fish at distance rather than trying to stalk them close to. This did not work particularly well: the sound of the bomb entering such a puddle alarmed them greatly. Also, the extreme shallowness and depth of silt made bait presentation like this very difficult indeed.

My solution was arrived at purely accidentally. The shallowness of the water and the abundance of the carp attracted a heron population and I set about trying to photograph the herons during their dawn fishing sessions. For this, I put up a small canvas hide for them to get used to so that I could take up residence unobserved with my cameras. It soon became obvious that it was not only the herons that became used to the canvas hide: the carp, too, began to accept it as part of the landscape.

After just a few days, I found it quite possible to sit in the hide, rod poking through and catch a carp from my very feet.

Clear Water and Natural Food

In 1979 some wild carp were moved again to a small clear moat that varied between two and twelve feet in depth. The fish flourished and began to grow again, but the clarity of the water and profusion of natural food made them very reluctant to accept normal baits. In fact, they carried their caution of bait and tackle with them to this new water and their memories proved to be very long indeed.

The solution was only a partial one. One summer evening, after a great deal of sun and a brisk breeze that died away in the late afternoon, a large slick of dead insects and general scum built up around the shallower part of the moat. By about eight o'clock this surface film was bulging with fish. Careful investigation showed that the wild carp were there in numbers, moving quite deliberately just sub-surface. Minute investigation showed that, in fact, these fish were taking hatching nymphs, or buzzers to coin a trout fisher's phrase, from the surface film itself. It would be nice to say that they fell for an artificial fly fished rainbow trout

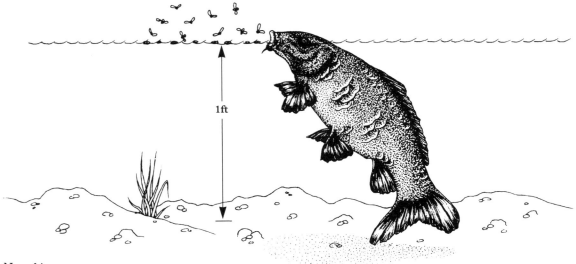

Nymphing carp.

Wildies are traditionally the old fully-scaled carp that so delighted our grandfathers.

A true wild carp is returned to a Welsh lake.

fashion. They might well have done, but I did not have trout tackle with me. What did catch two good wildies were dead moths, fished on size fourteen hooks, a yard away from very small controller floats. The moths were simply allowed to lie in the scum, twitched every now and again as a feeding carp approached. Not a practical solution for all carp in all waters in all weathers, but certainly proof that there is more than one way of killing a cat, as they say.

Chub

The marl pit had a stock of crucian carp, mostly very small but, rumour had it, with one or two decent fish. This was the attraction and these were the fish caught on light float tackle. The amazing thing was, however, that once every two or three sessions, the float would zing away and something would be attached to the end that would defy all pressure, angling skill and break the line within ten seconds! This happened again and again until, at last, a large chub was landed. This had to be the culprit and curiosity was satisfied – for a while.

Breakages still occurred all too frequently and the belief that this one chub was responsible began to appear more and more unlikely. As soon as the gear was stepped up in strength bites would cease altogether and neither the crucians nor the strange 'torpedoes' would show the slightest interest at all. A rod conventionally set up for carp remained fishless for days and so, with great reluctance, it was back to the old light line tactics.

The float flashed under in time-honoured fashion and the 'bullet' was felt. Immediately, the bail arm was whipped back and slack was given. A couple of yards out into the lake the float resurfaced and ambled, aimlessly around the open water. Once well away from the reeds that had proved constant sanctuary, pressure was put on again and this time, lured into a snag-free zone, the fish was just landed – a wild carp of 5lb 8oz, an almost impossible prize on 2lb bottom when fished close to reeds. Mind you, the technique takes nerve and is only successful about fifty per cent of the time.

A CRUCIAN CONUNDRUM

The Water

A three-acre farm pit, dug for irrigation purposes in the early 1980s, it was generally shallow but with a deeper central channel running down the spine of the water. It was surrounded by trees and had good weed growth, a proliferation of arrowhead-type lilies.

The Fish

The pit was stocked with swarms of tiny roach, rudd and hybrids, with a few smaller pike doing nothing to keep the numbers down. The target fish were very handsome crucian carp up to nearly four pounds. There were probably between sixty and eighty crucians in the pit.

The Problem

The problem was, quite simply, the mass of tiny fish. As we all know, large crucians are one of the wariest of carp types and need to be fished for with the most delicate of tackle and small, succulent baits. Whenever hemp, a grain of corn or a couple of maggots were introduced, the result was inevitable: a tiny roachling within seconds. Also, it was impossible to overfeed the small fish; heavy feeding simply attracted millions of them into the area. A hair-tearing problem for the serious crucian man.

The Solution

Unbelievably, these crucian have found their own way round a problem that is obviously a matter of life and death to them: they have changed from their normal pernickety crucian habits to feed exactly like their larger carp cousins. In fact, the larger the bait, the better. For example, as soon as large pieces of slowly sinking crust on a size six hook were used, eight crucians of over two pounds fell in an hour and a half. Obviously, in order to survive these crucians have become used to eating large

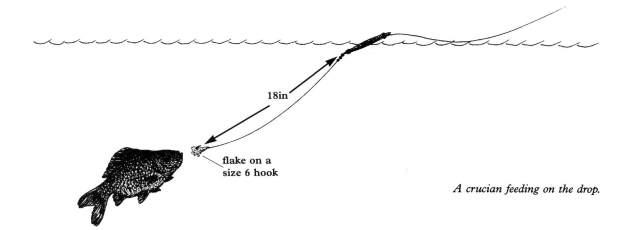

18in

flake on a
size 6 hook

A crucian feeding on the drop.

foodstuffs that the roach and rudd simply cannot handle.

A very small challenge indeed, but an interesting one which proves that hidebound thinking gets you nowhere in carping.

The New Problem

I wrote up this crucian challenge at the end of the 1991–92 season when I was quite smug about the water and felt that it was sorted out in every way. Summer 1993 was very different indeed. The weather was less warm and the weed growth on the lake was far more widespread, so much so that it was almost difficult to find a swim. All this need not have mattered too much, though. In fact, when I returned to the pit in July I confidently expected to repeat my successes of the previous year and approached the water in exactly the same way. I mixed up a bucket of lightly soaked bread and breadcrust, mingled with additives and a can of sweetcorn, and threw this out into thinner patches of weed. The water clouded nicely and the crust swam attractively in the surface currents. Everything went according to plan for a while; that is the small roach and rudd began to pour into the area and to attack the crusts and I certainly expected the crucians soon to follow. They did not; not that day, nor the next,

nor the next. Indeed, for one reason or another it seemed that the method was useless.

All this would not have been too bad if traditional crucian carp methods had worked. However, the pit proved to be an absolute swine and, to my knowledge, only a handful of crucians were caught through the rest of the summer, although one was a very large fish at over 4lb.

Early September found me looking round the pit for a solution, although I was not at all enthusiastic considering the cold weather and the heavy rainfalls that were so uncharacteristic of a normally pleasant time of the year.

Partial Solution Number 1

In fact, in a very short time it seemed as though the driving rain had actually worked to my advantage. All in all, in thirty-six hours over two inches of rain fell on to the land, into the feeder streams and flooded into the pit which rose, I guess, about eight or nine inches. The net effect of this was to swamp the weed and almost clear the surface. The weather grew significantly warmer after the deluge and the roach were noticeably more active on the surface.

A trip to the pit seemed in order and I began by feeding heavily with floating bread. This drew in the roach, but after only half an hour crucians began to move in and I caught two before dusk fell. I am sure that the raised water level played a dramatic part in this success; the fish were not as tight to the weedbeds and were moving around in open water as they had been doing in the summer of 1992. Fish mobility is obviously very important when it comes to the all-important question of finding surface baits. If the crucians are nested up in thick weed, the roach simply grind down the floating crust long before they even have an inkling it is out there.

However, this success was not to be repeated. The weather grew cold once more and fish disappeared from the surface. It was back, therefore, to the drawing-board again.

Partial Solution Number 2

I do not readily give up, especially when the prize of a 4lb crucian carp seemed so very close indeed. It was obviously necessary to go back on to the bottom and this took a good deal of thinking out and a lot of bankside observation. All the swims looked very attractive from the surface, but I knew that only a few held crucians in any number and it was imperative to watch for signs. Signs that, eventually, I found. After a couple of early morning visits I observed that one stretch of bank seemed to attract more activity than any other area. Frequent bursts of bubbles on both days and a handful of crucian sightings convinced me to give the area a try. I began by careful plumbing: the bottom shelved from four to eight feet very rapidly indeed and then levelled off. That shelf appeared to be very clean and was probably being browsed by travelling fish.

Bait would be a problem. Anything small would be picked up, but I had little faith in anything too large (apart from breadflake) as crucians like to suck and blow at smaller food items. In the end I settled on corn again, but decided to dye it red and flavour it with Scopex – a tip I had received from Archie Braddock. Although this book does not deal with baits in depth but concentrates on other facets of the art, in this situation the colouring and/or the flavouring worked very well indeed for me. For a couple of days I fed in free samples of corn and on the third evening visited the lake as the daylight began to wander into night. In two hours I had taken three crucians – all good fish – and for the first time in 1993 felt some confidence that a problem had at least been partially solved.

THE WONDER POT

Every now and again an unexpected and seemingly trivial piece of tackle can work wonders and do something for you that you would never guess. Such was the case with the wonder pot.

The Water

The River Bure is just about as strange a carp water as you would ever expect to find. It rises in mid North Norfolk and runs for a good few miles as a trout river. By the time it reaches Aylsham it is wide and deep and has to some extent become more placid; it is now the home of good roach, bream, chub, pike and perch. However, it is still, definitely, not seen as a carp water.

The Fish

So how did carp get into this river and how many of them are there? I cannot answer either question with complete confidence, but I have my suspicions. Many years ago I dug two carp lakes that were connected by a long and winding stream to the headwaters of the river itself. On a couple of occasions these lakes flooded and very small carp were washed down the stream and, I am fairly confident, into the river. A few of them colonized a small lake in Itteringham and grew, I believe, to a reasonable size. However, of carp in the river itself I heard nothing at all for many years. Then, on an exploratory trip for roach in 1993, I saw a very good-looking fish below Buxton, many miles from Itteringham. It was obviously alone and could conceivably have been the only one left in the river, although there was a long stretch of slower deeper water beneath where I saw it so I cannot be sure on that point.

The Problem

At first the problem did not seem too great: I wanted to catch the fish to see if it was from my lake. Of course, definite proof would be impossible, but the fish that I had reared did have various distinguishing marks, generally in the shape of very noticeable scale patterns, and I was quite keen to see if this fish fitted for my own nostalgic reasons.

Everything seemed to be very easy indeed. I soon had the carp taking sweetcorn on a gentle gravel run and after only an hour managed to put a hook into it. It went off with a predictably strong rush and the sturdy chub tackle that I had with me at the time was simply not up to the job. The carp buried in runuculous weed and that was the end of that, even though I began to wade the river to get a different angle of pull on it.

A few days later the fish had deserted the open water, but I found it hemmed in under a length of alder and willow trees. It would take food underneath them, but no way would it come out into open water. The lesson had obviously been learned. More worrying was the fact that the carp lay a good ten yards into the tree cover and there was no way of placing a bait at all close that I could see. This truly seemed to be the carp that got away.

A shot going back over the years: one of my small carp lies dead, stabbed by a heron.

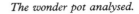

The wonder pot analysed.

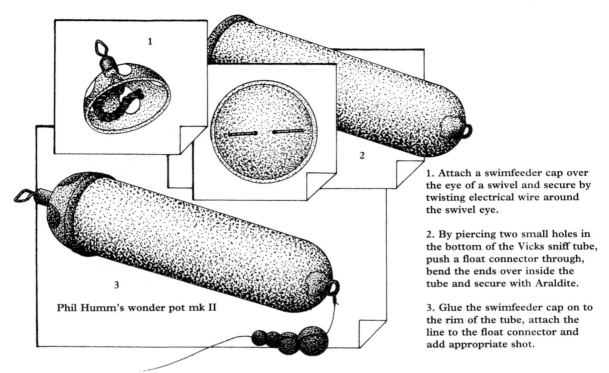

Phil Humm's wonder pot mk II

1. Attach a swimfeeder cap over the eye of a swivel and secure by twisting electrical wire around the swivel eye.

2. By piercing two small holes in the bottom of the Vicks sniff tube, push a float connector through, bend the ends over inside the tube and secure with Araldite.

3. Glue the swimfeeder cap on to the rim of the tube, attach the line to the float connector and add appropriate shot.

The Solution

Then I remembered the wonder pot. The diagram above says all you need to know about its structure. The design and the wonder pot I used were both sent to me by Phil Humm, that inventive, ambitious angler from Essex. Together with the tool came a letter saying:

We use the wonder pot on a normal running leger-type set-up. You cast it gently and with very little practice you can make it trot down a swim beneath all the overhanging branches or to a desired gap in the streamer weed. A quick jab on the rod tip turns it sideways, at which point it fills up and sinks exactly at the desired spot. It has been very successful on the Lea for chub and on swims that everyone walks past. If they do try to fish their bait ends up far too far away from the fish for a take.

So, armed with the wonder pot I sallied forth to the Bure again, this time with tackle better equipped for the job. As Phil said, the wonder pot was easy to cast, easy to control and sank exactly where I had marked the carp down. A few minutes after casting the rod tip pulled round very confidently and soon I was gazing at a fish that I was sure was one of my own babies from years ago.

Certainly, the wonder pot is a gimmick, but it just proves that tackle innovation is always important.

THE CANAL CARP

The Water

The word canal is really a misnomer: in fact, all I am talking about is a strip of water about a mile long that runs between two lakes, connecting them rather like an elongated hourglass. The canal is very shallow, anything from mere inches to a couple of feet and about five to eight yards wide. The sides are fringed in reeds and the bottom is mainly accumulated silt with patches of bared stone and gravel. Both the lakes in question are eighteenth century in origin and the canal was constructed at the same time, around 1780. There is frequent algae growth, but at times the water becomes crystal clear. There is very little bottom weed of any description.

The Fish

Occasionally bream make their way from the lakes into the canal, stop there for a while and then move on again, but this is rare. There are a few shoals of roach that travel the length of the canal but even they tend to keep away as the place is the haunt of herons. The carp in question number about forty fish and are long, lean commons that have been in the water for many years and are very similar to large wild carp. The smallest fish are probably between 5lb and 8lb with some of the larger ones edging towards mid-doubles. They appear to be quite old fish and going nowhere, particularly, in terms of size. But this does not detract from their interest, beauty or fighting ability which is quite extraordinary in such shallow water.

The Problem

The water is so shallow and so clear that it might not exist at all. It really is as though those carp are hanging in air rather than water. This means that bait presentation is very difficult; certainly line is almost immediately spied out and the carp will quickly leave any area that has a float or line showing on the surface or in mid-water. Although the fish are not heavily pressured, they are able to see anything untoward from a distance and avoid the swim. However, they are very partial to particle baits.

The Solution

Within that last sentence lies the solution. The good thing about particle baits is that they can stir fish up into a feeding frenzy. In this shallow canal hemp, casters, maggots and sweetcorn all serve the same function: put enough particles in and the carp will begin to burrow and throw up silt-clouds. They do not lose caution, so the approach must be very careful. However, the result of all their burrowing is to make the water very cloudy and it is this fish-created murkiness that effectively masks the line and even a float. The answer is, therefore, to bait a couple of places and wait until the fish move in and thoroughly muddy the entire area. Then, and only then, can the bait and tackle be introduced and be acceptable.

Of course, this canal is to some extent a 'one-off'. However, the principle is a sound one in shallow clear waters. If enough bait can be introduced – particles particularly – that the clarity is destroyed, the fishing is that much easier. I suspect that is why raking the bottom for tench has proved to be so effective. The old idea that natural food is grubbed up and this excites the tench is, I think, wrong. What the raking does is to cloud a clear water and give the tench more security and confidence when feeding. Obviously, the use of a rake would be disastrous in most carp-fishing situations but it is, you see, possible to get the fish to do the same job for you by themselves.

Carp go mad for particles.

PHIL'S RIVER CARP

Phil Humm is more than a mere inventor of gadgets and contraptions and is, in fact, one of the breed of new young anglers who will surely step into the shoes of the declining generation! Here he describes an opportunistic capture of a river common.

The Water

Kings Weir on the Lea was, until a few years ago, a manual weir operated by the late Bill Newton, but it is now automatic. The water flowed over from the canal, but the weirpool is still beautiful and in years gone by people fished from punts under the sill for barbel or with silkweed as bait for roach. This was the stamping ground of a very young Fred Crouch before he turned his attention to the Royalty with such devastating effect. Sadly, nowadays the pool is monopolized by a few barbel anglers, satisfied with catching the same fish over and over again.

The barbel grow big, with a number of doubles to potentially over 12lb and chub historically to over 6lb. Fortunately, because the really big barbel stay in the pool, the river does not receive as much sustained pressure as it possibly deserves. The stretch I fish starts where the river flows out of the pool. It is wide, fast and gravelly, with streamer weed, but it quickly slows up as it deepens, despite narrowing. The swim I eventually caught the carp from is the second down, about fifty yards from the end of the pool. It is called, not very originally, the Top Tree Swim.

The river deepens off into a number of swims on a walled section where the river is artificially straightened and deepened to provide water in a drought. These are good winter swims and I took my first 5lb chub and double-figure barbel from here. The river then hits a bridge and shallows up, again barbel country. I have had some great fun watching fish off the bridge and, just below, catching chub on slugs and worms while fishing from trees or in the deep undergrowth.

The pit is large, over a hundred acres, and dotted with islands and runs parallel with the river down that stretch. On the day I caught the carp I had been fishing the pit all night. I had seen a shoal of bream and some of them looked pretty decent. However, I had not had a take all night and not even seen a tench. At

about half past nine I packed up and left a little platform I had built. It was a glorious morning.

The Fish

To leave the fishery I had to walk downstream, over a bridge and back upstream. I always put my polaroids on because you never know what you will spot and I am the eternal optimist. The riverside is thick with crack-willow, elderflower, mulberry and all manner of foliage. Right at the top of the stretch I spotted the carp.

It was in a swim made by the regular barbel anglers encouraging a tree to bend over the water. They were a little too enthusiastic, however, and it went right into the water with its stump sticking out in mid-river. As you can guess, I dropped my gear and watched the fish. It was stuck tight into the slack behind the

The carp shows clearly lying in the shelter of its snag swim.

stump and I could see it very well from the high bank. I had a loaf of bread and although I did not think I stood a chance I went downstream and started flicking small pieces past the snag with the catapult. How much reaction? Zero!

The Problem and the Solution

It is my experience that carp or any fish, however wary, can normally be brought round to a simple bait subject to a number of conditions. They must not know that you are there, they must be in a 'safe' area and you must not introduce feed too heavily, rather just a little at a time. I remember under these conditions having virtually every carp feeding under my nose on corn, in a lake where it was supposed to be so hard that you should forget it before you begin!

I had not really thought about how I would present the bait and the sun was climbing higher all the time. However, I had nothing in particular to go home for and the fishery was very quiet and peaceful, so I just kept introducing the flake and watching it float into the eddy and eventually downriver.

Finally, I got a reaction as the fish slipped into the flow and, mesmerized, followed a piece down for about ten yards. The fish was shocked when it realized how far from home it was and shot back into the eddy. Three or four more pieces and it just tipped up and sucked a piece in – brilliant! – but it would not get into a frenzy and just took occasionally. I was just about to give up when two more smaller fish turned up and introduced competition. It was not long before I had all three of the carp chasing the bread everywhere.

Now I had to put a plan together. The fishing position is dominated by the huge willow bush

Phil proudly holds a beautiful example of a fully-scaled carp.

in front and after going down some steps you cannot even see the snag where the fish was holed up. I set up a 1½lb, 11ft rod with no weight on the line and tied on a size eight. It was an Aitkim pattern with a very slight out-point. Quite why I did this I do not know, but during the close-season I had taken some hooks and superglued a thin streak of cork to the outside of the shank. This enabled me to free-line the flake but pinch it really hard to provide casting weight, and *still* it floated. I tested it first in the water and was completely happy with it.

I had to get into a position where I could cast to the fish and this meant creeping into the water and edging downstream until I could just see it. At this stage I guessed I would only get one cast and that had to be correct first time. The real hurdle would be putting the bait into the eddy and keeping it there just long enough to get a take. The flow came down both sides of the snag, and even if I got the bait into position the push on the line would pull it straight out and off down the stream far too quickly for carp to take. So I hung the line, first cast over the furthest twig of the willow that was now upstream of me. I hit the eddy perfectly and the line fluttered down on to the leaf. It was beautiful; I had about two inches of line on the water keeping everything out of the flow. It took a few seconds to adjust the position, then the carp tipped up and took the bait down. It was one of those situations where the fish simply had no suspicion and I had plenty of time to strike, literally watching the line come out of the fish's mouth. After much mayhem and root diving the carp was in the net. It was a fabulous mahogany common, a real joy to cradle. Then, home for Sunday lunch!

PETER SMITH'S SURFACE CHALLENGE

Peter Smith is an extraordinarily accomplished angler and it is surprising that his name is not more widely known in angling circles. He has an exceptional record of big carp and barbel and has fished for over twenty years with the likes of Yates, James and Ashby. Barbel on the Welsh borderlands where he owns a country house hotel now take up most of his time and interest, but carp remain very dear to him. This challenge dates back many years and relates to a very rich water which was considered imposs-ible on the surface. Indeed, rich waters often respond only very slowly indeed to surface-fished baits and sometimes not at all. Here is Peter's story.

The Water

The lake is not particularly large, is generally very clear and exceptionally rich. There is one weed-bed, of fully grown lilies, that is so big that it dominates the entire lake. Carp are the most exciting fish in the water, both mirrors and commons and twenty-pounders are far from unusual, in fact are even probably the norm. Thirty-pounders have been caught and certainly fish well over forty pounds have been seen. The water, therefore, has both enormous potential and charm.

The Problem

The lake is one of those fortunate places that do not come under a great deal of pressure; in fact the syndicate only boasts six members and many of them fish only irregularly. Probably because of this, the carp did not see many floating baits and refused them if they did appear. In short, the water got the reputation for being impossible off the top and few, if any, of the syndicate members even bother to try further.

The Solution

Peter's firm theory is that carp will always feed best in that area of the lake where access to them is the hardest and certainly where it is impossible to put up a bivvy! You do need a tent or an umbrella or some other shelter for a long stay, but the thing to do is to keep moving as soon as daylight cracks. On the particular day in question, it was apparent that there were a great number of carp way out, right in the centre of the lily-bed. Peter had read in one of Jack Hilton's books or articles that 18lb line could cut through lily stems and not be broken. Peter's mind was made up. For some time he catapulted Chum Mixers, then a relatively new bait, out into the very middle of the most thickly weeded area. Nothing happened for a while, but eventually the carp got a taste for the Mixers. Hand-sized mouths appeared. Heads knocked the Chum Mixers off the lilypads. There was no doubt that the carp could sense the presence of the food through the vegetation. All the Mixers on the fringes of the lilies were ignored and those in open water simply washed in slowly towards the bank. It hardly mattered; Peter had his 18lb line and put his trust in it.

The first fish was hooked. Peter simply held tight, not allowing the fish to dive into the lily roots. This is vital. If you keep the pressure constant and unrelenting, the fish will do all the work for you and actually work itself clear of the lilies, forcing a path through them. It is vital not to let the fish get down to the roots, where not even 18lb line will cut.

In that single session Peter took three carp of over 20lb. It was one of those days when everything fell into place and went right. It was a case of putting together two or three pieces of information to come up with the correct solution to an irritating problem. Although that was some time ago, Peter's approach would not change now and in fact does not when he is faced with a difficult water. The 18lb line would now perhaps be replaced by Big Game 20lb strength, but even the bait would probably remain the same.

THE CARP AT PEG 22

It is a frequent mistake to think that carp in

A beautiful carp taken at close range just sub-surface.

some ways belong to the specialist rather than to the common man. Of course, the vast majority of those very big fish fall to those anglers dedicated to their capture, but not all of them. Carp mean a great deal to a great many anglers, matchmen included.

Ron Lees is far more than a matchman, he is the complete freshwater fisherman who transcends all the false boundaries we like to try to put up around the sport. The carp in this, Ron's story, is not huge, but the challenge set by the fish was significant and the solution emphasizes at least two important truths about the behaviour of the species. Ron describes the episode that follows as a real sporting game with the fish that led him and many others quite a dance for over two years.

Peg 22.

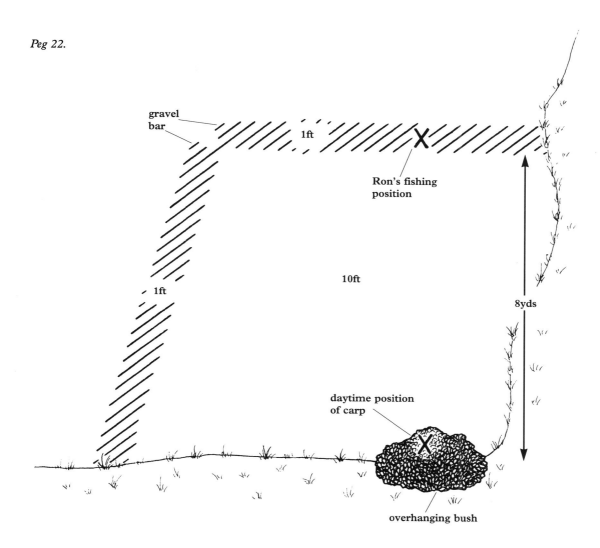

gravel bar

1ft

1ft

Ron's fishing position

10ft

8yds

daytime position of carp

overhanging bush

The Water

Upton Warren gravel pit is about eighteen acres and is generally a pea-green colour, probably because of the influx of nitrates from the surrounding land. It is spring-fed, but even these springs are likely to be tainted by the amount of agricultural pollution that has gone on for some years. Other fish in the water include crucian carp and some very large roach, most of these stocked a few years before the time of this story to over 3lb.

The Fish and the Problem

The carp that we are talking about was not particularly large, but for well over two years it destroyed the hopes and the tackle of many of the matchmen that fished on Peg 22. Peg 22 is right on a corner of the gravel pit and it is hedged in almost entirely by a very shallow gravel bar running about eight yards out that really fences the swim in entirely. The swim itself is about ten feet deep but the gravel bar is only inches and the water drops away steeply once again on the other side towards the middle of the pit. The focal point of this corner swim is a large bush almost directly on the corner, the one piece of shelter that attracts the majority of the fish.

It became almost usual for a matchman to hook this carp at some point during the match, but the story was invariably the same: after an initial plunge towards the roots of the bush, the carp would turn towards the middle of the pit, and the more the angler tried to put on pressure, the harder the carp would accelerate. Match-gear, being what it is, invariably found the pressure too much to cope with and the carp would either break before reaching the gravel bar or very shortly afterwards. Ron himself hooked the carp three times in a match, the first time on light pole tackle and the second time on main lines of 2½lb breaking strain. Despite this step-up in line strength there was still nothing he could do once the carp had made his mind up.

The Solution

Once again Ron was drawn in Peg 22, but this time he had thought out a plan to the conundrum. First, he took his basket out from the right-hand bank, along the bar and placed it on the gravel itself. At first the basket floated and he had to weight it down with a number of bricks. Next, he stepped up his gear to a quite strong 13½ft match rod and 2.6lb line straight through to two casters on a size sixteen hook fished under a waggler.

He began to bait the bush very heavily, knowing that he would have to put the bait right under the branches if he was going to pull the carp out at all. He knew that the carp spent the daytime hours almost exclusively under the branches of the tree and never ventured more than a foot or so out into open water, unless hooked.

He fed carefully and crucian carp began to come to the net. Then, at last, the float dipped in a decisive way and he knew that the moment had come. At this point Ron realized that the more you put pressure on a fish, the more it is

likely to try to swim away from you. For this reason Ron actively pulled the fish towards the bar, suspecting that the fish would react by remaining in the deep pocket of water close to the bank. He was proved right. The carp did nothing particularly dramatic, but simply plugged around in the deep water for one hour and fifteen minutes. At last it began to roll and Ron was able to get off his basket, wade down the gravel shelf and finally net it.

The carp weighed 10lb 6oz, enough to win Ron a fair amount of prize money. On the opposite bank lies a nature reserve with water cordoned off from the main pit. After the match Ron carried the big fish to the reserve and slipped it in there. Thankfully, as far as match anglers are concerned, it has not been seen since!

Those two truths? Firstly, in the daylight, a carp will very often take up residence in a certain snag or under a certain bush and not move at all until darkness falls. Secondly, the more you put strain on a fish, the more it will battle against that strain. Play a fish more gently and you might well be able to tease it away from trouble.

MATTHEW CHAPMAN'S TEST CHALLENGE

Matthew is a shining example of our up-and-coming anglers. Recently he sent me a quite magical book on carp fishing, privately produced, entitled *A Never Forgotten Dawn*. This small book was so sensitive and so thoughtful that I realized at once that a real new talent had emerged and I got in touch with him immediately. Matthew is twenty-five, a history teacher and obviously knows his Wessex waters exceptionally well. Here is his fascinating account of some of the most unusual carp I personally have ever heard of, although knowing the species' amazing adaptability, I am not in the least surprised that they thrive in this extraordinary habitat.

Matthew with his 10lb mirror, immaculate in every way.

The Water

In the Test valley lies a fish farm, beneath this fish farm is a lagoon and from this lagoon runs a crystal-clear, gushing chalk stream of some fifty or a hundred yards. This stream then enters the main body of an equally gin-clear lake of about three and a half acres. This all represents a quite unique environment that is extraordinarily rich and very difficult to fish.

The Fish

These are young carp from mixed parentage but several, apparently, have been reared from the Leney strain. The biggest of them are now topping 20lb, which is extraordinary considering how young they are and how small they were stocked. The fish tend to wander from

the lake up the stream through the lagoon right to the fringes of the trout farm itself. Perhaps stray pellets from the farm help to explain the fabulous growth rates, but then again this is the Test valley where plants, weed and trout all grow fantastically well. Also, remember that the carp were carefully chosen and the waters are equally carefully managed.

The Problem

The problems are many and varied. One major problem is the extremely nomadic nature of the fish, that are almost like barbel in the way that they are very happy in the fastest of currents. They also tend to lurk under branches, rafts and small bridges, again in barbel fashion.

Also consider how clear the water is. This breeds an extreme wariness in the fish that tend to pop like corks out of champagne bottles at the first sign of an angler.

Then there is the problem of their feeding habits. How these fish survive is almost a puzzle, and Matthew has only seen them feed in traditional wallowing carp fashion once in the lake. It would appear that they browse little and often, from natural food sources only.

The problem of location is a strange one as it appears that the carp here can melt almost into nothingness. Matthew has seen them push into the silt of the lake until they were absolutely invisible from just a few yards with polaroid glasses in crystal-clear water.

Yet another problem is the fact that the fishery owner is an experienced carp man himself and knows all the problems that modern baits and methods can bring to carp. As a result he has put several sane restrictions on the anglers: no boilies can be used and bolt-rigs and hair-rigs are banned. Particles are also restricted and the only baits really viable are naturals or meat or bread or trout pellet paste. These baits in themselves attract another problem – trout! The water is full of them and worms will be bolted down and even floated crust accounted for a five-pounder.

Several demoralizing episodes took place. For example, one afternoon Matthew sat in the branches of a tree which had fallen over the stream, gradually feeding a carpet of luncheon meat into the swim. There were carp cruising four feet beneath him and yet not a single fish even looked at the meat once. In fact, it was another week of using meat before a fish even followed a piece to the bottom and then it did not take.

The Solutions

Like the problems, there is not really one simple straightforward solution here: rather Matthew was forced into all manner of ruses and tricks to winkle carp out. The first fish came from beneath a bridge over the stream, really just a piece of grating. As Matthew crept out he saw a carp's head poking barbel-fashion out of the bridge, pointing, obviously, upstream. For a few minutes he fed maggots into the current until the fish became agitated and began picking off the odd one as it floated by. He then put on a small worm weighted with a shot and let that trundle to the feeding carp. It was taken. The fight as you can imagine was vigorous, even if the fish was 'only' a 5lb mirror. Size, on this type of challenge, is unimportant.

This episode obviously reinforced the theory that the carp would be vulnerable to naturals. The next success came when Matthew was hidden at the head of the stream. A shoal of seven fish slowly came out of the lake towards him, apparently feeding on something. Between him and the fish was a gravel hump in the stream and on to this he cast another worm which rose and fell in the current. The 'Magnificent Seven' drew close and one of them went over. In the gin-clear water, Matthew could see its gills opening and closing. The strike proved that the second fish was on its way to the net, but not before it cleared the water just like a fresh round salmon. That fish was again a mirror but this time a double at 10lb 8oz.

Matthew's history on the water has been like this, picking off odd fish as he has built up more and more knowledge about the fish's habits. As he says, in such a water it is possible to learn more in one session than in a season on a more conventional lake. For example, he got to know one fish that had such a fixed patrol route that you could even set your watch by it: it travelled the same way to a rigid schedule and went down to feed at the same spot every time. Matthew started to introduce broad beans (one of the allowed particles) into this area and he noticed that the fish would pick up just one broad bean each time, ignoring the others and thus cutting down his chances of being hooked tremendously. In the end, Matthew began to fish a single broad bean with no prebaiting whatsoever.

He has also begun to pin-point other feeding areas, mostly unusual ones and often in the stream, tight in to the margins. Mass baiting

Early morning success.

with maggots can be the key to success in these sort of areas; mass baiting is important as it tends to feed the trout off and allow the carp a chance. As you would expect, the carp seem to be drawn to gravel slopes and these areas are the ones that Matthew prebaits the heaviest.

This is probably the greatest lesson to learn from this particular challenge: carp may move a good deal during the course of their normal working day but frequently they will only feed on very isolated areas of the bottom. In many cases it is essential to work out exactly where these are. A bait just a yard or two out of a hot area will not even be seen, never mind picked up. This is the beauty of tight, clear waters, everything can be seen and the mind can really click into gear.

7 IT'S THE LITTLE THINGS . . .

Many years ago, when I was a schoolteacher, I used to run a fishing club and one of the highlights was the springtime when we could move on to fly fishing. This was an area that was new to most of the boys and they relished it. Watching beginners fish is rarely gripping but in this case it was very interesting indeed because I began to realize that the tiniest thing could mean the difference between success and failure and that very often a boy needed to be doing something only minutely wrong to go home fishless. Often, for example, a cast knot was simply too clumsy and created a wake in the water that alarmed the trout. Sometimes the fly was tied to the line improperly so that it hung incorrectly and was fished with a dubious action: again no trout. On and on went that list, and I came to realize that it was only the boys who got ninety-five per cent of the things right who caught any fish at all. One seemingly insignificant detail overlooked and that was the end of things.

It is exactly the same when fishing with a bait, but somehow it does not seem quite as immediately obvious. Certainly, in carp fishing the smallest detail can prove absolutely central to the entire operation. What I have done here is to select a few pictures that illustrate this particular point. There is no bragging here – far from it, for often I was doing something stupidly wrong in the first place! The attempt is simply to try to make you think all the time – or at least, that is, when you are not actually catching. Carp are not all geniuses and if you are not putting them on the bank then you are probably doing something wrong: often not much wrong and something that could be remedied very quickly and easily indeed.

The photograph opposite (top) takes us back quite a long time to a little club water in East Anglia that was very heavily stocked with small to medium fish. However, it was very heavily pressured and things could get quite difficult there, especially during the daytime. I had been legering pieces of luncheon meat in the open water to the left of the trees straight in front of me. However, it was quite obvious that the carp were having nothing to do with the baits and were probably aware of the whole approach. What I did was simply to put on a float, strip off all lead and attach a piece of luncheon meat to a size 6 hook. This was cast right under the willows and the float simply sat on the weed. Now the line went vertically rather than at an angle through the water and was well hidden by weed anyway. Bites were almost instant and I am seen here playing one of the best of the day.

The photograph opposite (bottom), also going back a fair few years, shows David Judge unhooking a 20lb fish for me – quite a relief after a very frustrating morning. I had been clipped up very tight but occasionally had been aware of some activity at the rod tip that never developed. I simply unclipped and began to watch the line where it entered the water: whenever it lifted I hit it, however slight the movement, and this was the first fish to come to the net after a couple of abortive strikes. I went on to catch another four fish that day.

I am very proud of the fish that was landed in the photograph on page 140 (top). As you can see, the water was very low indeed and equally clear and for several days the fish had proved to be exceptionally spooky of all breaking strain lines even when they were hanging

Berni Neave – that excellent crucian catcher – watches John Bailey in action.

The fruits of pre-baiting with boilies.

limp. In the end I realized that fish were hanging around the island and I walked out to it with the bait and placed the boilie in close. Then, by hand, I hid the line under leaves and silt for at least twenty yards before coming back to the rods. I had a bite (the first for four days) within an hour and a quarter and finally landed a good mid-twenty.

The smile in the photograph on page 140 (bottom) says it all! It had been a harrowing day, for I had lost two good fish in the heavy weed a few yards out. Obviously a change of gear was called for and I upped both line and hook strength. The problem was that the carp would no longer suck the corn and a heavy hook into their mouths even though they continued to feed, passing over the bait frequently. Some polystyrene would have done the trick but I did not have any, so I grubbed about in the undergrowth and found a small worm which I hooked next to the corn as a type of cocktail. This was taken almost instantly and I

John Bailey fights to control a big fish taken at distance.

The smile says it all!

can only assume that the carp saw the worm and sucked more violently than it had been doing for the corn alone. Perhaps this was all a fluke, but it is a manœuvre that has worked for me a few times since then.

The fish in the photograph opposite (left) really pleased me as it was one of my first serious estate lake twenties. After having been successful with maggots I had begun using them here, but had great trouble getting actual bites. This fish fell to three casters on a size 8 hook placed over a maggot bed. I think two things worked in my favour: firstly, the casters counteracted the weight of the hook which was important, but secondly (and perhaps even more significant), the carp were probably picking out the casters as especially attractive titbits.

Old wildies, like that in the photograph opposite (right), are never easy and this one fell for a worm twitched very energetically every minute or so. There is no doubt (for I saw it all) that this hopping movement caught the eye

In the net . . . a good 'twenty'.

One of the old fully scaled commons pretty well now dead and gone from the Boathouse lake.

of the browsing fish which hurried over to investigate. Hurry is precisely the word to use here as, for once, it failed to show any real caution and sucked the bait in without any investigation whatsoever. Normally I would hesitate before using a technique like this but perhaps an energetic worm is not that uncommon on the lake bed.

The fish in the photograph on page 142 (top) meant an awful lot to me because it came on a return visit to a beloved lake where I had been successful before on sweetcorn. The bait now seemed to be useless and fish either ignored it or showed some signs of alarm when going over it. I persevered, however, and began to introduce more rather than less corn. After a while this seemed to swing the balance and a few fish began to feed on it again. Once they started so did the others, and I found that once

more corn was a killing bait. I hold the proof.

The super fish in the photograph on page 142 (bottom) came from the same campaign but illustrates yet another aspect. You will notice on the right a heavy fringe of overhanging trees. All the bait (either freebies or hookbait) had to be placed within a yard or 4ft (1.2m) at the most from these trees. There was a long stretch of clear sand and gravel where it was obvious the fish had been feeding and you had to get right in on this or face innumerable blanks. Six inches (15cm) the wrong side would have meant failure – it was as simple as that.

No enormous amount of thought was needed in any of these cases and yet each time a good fish came as a result of a fairly limited development. I suppose the message is not to despair with your whole approach if things are not going quite right, but just think how to

A majestic fish from a magnificent setting.

Again the Boathouse figures along with a bull-shouldered fish taken in torrential rain.

modify it a little and the results might well happen. As, indeed they have for many more of my friends.

THAT FINAL FINISHING TOUCH by Matt Hayes

I can recall many examples in my angling career when a small change of rig or terminal tackle transformed poor or mediocre results into spectacular successes. Typically, it happened quite recently during a summer campaign on a difficult carp water. The lake in question is a large, mature gravel pit with a small head of carp, the majority of which are commons with an average size of 14lb to 18lb. Although the pit does not seem to contain giants, its attraction is the sheer quality of the fish, many of which have

never been caught before. Furthermore, I was privileged enough to be fishing the lake virtually alone.

After a few, inevitable blank sessions, I identified one swim in particular that began to produce the odd carp. It centred around a plateau 65yd (59m) from the bank, the area around which was heavily weeded, as were the sides, with Canadian pondweed with liberal quantities of soft silkweed draped around like candyfloss. The obvious area to place the bait was actually on the plateau itself, as anywhere else it would be likely to be hidden. The plateau was also located directly on the carp's major patrol route and was an obvious ambush point. It was clearly a favourite feeding area, judging by the lack of weed.

I discovered, though, that the plateau was only a temporary feeding area and that it

Matt Hayes holds a stunning common carp.

was impossible to persuade carp to stay on it for long periods. Rather, a fish or two could be caught before the group continued on its journey around the lake.

It was obvious from the outset that what I had to do was to stop carp in their tracks and I felt that bait choice was critical. I deliberately selected a bright, obvious boilie with the most appealing smell and taste that I could conjure up. The base mix was Dave Thorpe's Supercede (dayglow yellow) and Hutchinson's Scopex blended with Martin Locke's Pear of Bananas. The finished bait looked so good that I could have eaten it myself, as I often did when I forgot my sandwiches! The rig I chose was a straightforward 'in the line' lead type with a 12in hook length of 15lb Kryston Merlin. A standard bottom bait fished on a shortish hair completed the set-up. Both rods were fished the same way and cast on to the plateau and my usual tactic was to use approximately a hundred free baits, topped up with a further thirty if fish were caught.

Results using these tactics were mediocre and only occasional fish came along. The changes I made were very simple but highly effective, because I refined both the rig and the baiting programme. The rig change was simple. Instead of fishing a bottom bait I changed to a single, large pop-up, fished over a bed of smaller 14mm size boilies. I also used a 'swimmer rig' with the bait popped up some 2in (5cm) off the bottom. The other major difference was in the quantity of bait I used. On arrival, three hundred boilies were immediately fired out and after catching a carp I began topping up with a hundred freebies. The effect was dramatic, multiple catches of three, four or even five fish became common. I finished that year having caught most of the pit's residents – big, brassy common carp to over 20lb – proof indeed that a final, finishing touch can transform a campaign.

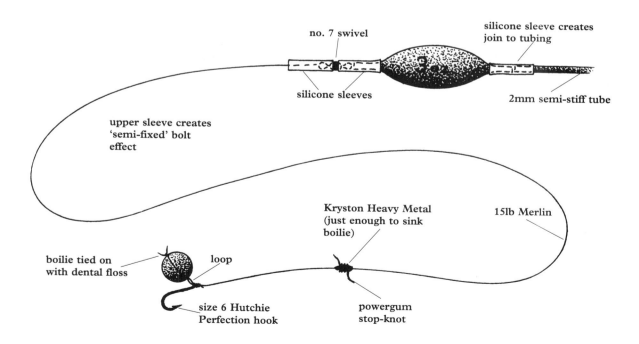

The swimmer set-up.

A CHANGE OF LUCK
by William (Bill) Whiting

Some would say that the reason for me experiencing a phenomenal number of blank sessions during the winter months over recent years is because I am getting old! However, I prefer to think this is not the case because although I am nearly sixty-seven, I have learnt a great deal over the years and there are very few who are as dedicated to carp fishing at my age. Let me tell you about one particular occasion and you can make your own mind up.

I was fishing at Waveney Valley Lakes many years ago on C lake where the roots and brambles below the surface were always favourite places for the carp. They felt comparatively safe there and obviously liked the underwater scenery too! It was winter and everywhere was clad in thick white frost which gave great beauty to a scene that was usually desolate at that time of the year. In spite of the cold there was no wind and the sun was shining, so that it was quite bearable. I soon settled down to fish very close to a large bramble bush that seemed to thrive even below the water line at the narrow end of the lake, where the depth was about 6ft (1.8m). That particular morning I was completely alone and as happy as could be.

I kept getting takes on almost every cast that took the bobbin up about 4in (10cm) and then stopped. On striking I failed to make contact each time and the hook just came out of the water into the branches around me. After many attempts without any success I became frustrated and imagined that the carp were just sucking the bait up to their lips without taking the hook in. At least from the action I was getting, it was obvious that the carp liked the bait.

Just by way of experimentation, I changed from size 6 hooks to size 2 hooks and the side-hooked boilie looked very odd indeed. I began to wonder, in fact, if I was resorting to foolish ideas in my desperation. However, within the next quarter of an hour I had caught and

Bill Whiting with a beautifully conditioned winter fish.

returned two fine carp into double figures and while I was unhooking the second actually had a run on the other rod which a friend struck, hooked and landed for me. He was absolutely astounded at so much action.

Looking back, perhaps those unhittable takes that I had experienced at first were carp sucking and blowing at the bait, and the heavier hook that I moved on to counteracted the misses by pulling the bait lower down into the mouth and making ejection much more difficult. Also, the fact that the hook-point was standing much further out from the bait probably helped as well. So, unlikely as the set-up looked, it certainly did work a miracle on that particular cold winter's day.

A CHANGE OF PLAN SAVES THE DAY by Mick Wood

It was with some enthusiasm that I drove down to the river in the dying days of the season. The winter had been very kind to me and produced chub fishing to the standard for which Yorkshire is rightly famous. Today, however, it seemed that I had asked for just one favour too many. Any hopes of a grand finale had been washed away by twelve feet of amber water spewing from the fells and, as I stood awe-struck at the mile-wide river, my mind raced through the alternatives that might salvage the day. The idea that I might try for carp nudged its head to the front of the field. I had never carp fished beyond the September deadline set by most decent men, even in these enlightened times, and I had always left such ventures to the heroes who fished the big pit over on the East Riding.

However, I observed around me the tell-tale signs of an early spring and began to perspire slightly in the mid-March sun, so the idea progressed from the possible to the probable; after all, who does not feel optimism when spring comes early? I quickly surveyed the contents of my bag. The garlic sausage would do fine and the 6lb line on the '300' would be ideal in a weed-free pool. My 12ft barbel rod, I knew from experience of many summer carp sessions, would serve me well as a float rod. A float! My goodness, a float! A short detour to the tackle shop and my kit was complete.

I had never set eyes upon Red Roofs Pool beyond the summer months. Its barren expression made it appear larger than its two acres and far less welcoming. The old wind pump and the flat surrounding fields of the Plain of York betrayed its original use as a source of irrigation. I surveyed the water, hoping for inspiration, but with no lily-fringed bays or leaf-shaded corners to catch eye or fish, I settled for where the water was deepest close in. The daylight hours were still too short to lift the water temperature noticeably and so a

Mick Wood and his winter wonder fish.

depth of 9ft (2.7m) at the rod tip seemed a good bet. The loaded waggler was set inches over depth and a BB pinched a foot above the hook. The morsel of garlic sausage was surrounded by a few dozen tiny particles of the same and the trap was set.

The river man who touch legers need never look at his rod and so the whole vista of the winter waterscape can be enjoyed. I found it difficult, therefore, to concentrate on the float and it was fortunate that the silver of red slipped quietly away sooner rather than later. An instinctive strike, a heartwarming battle and a low sun highlighted the golden flanks of a 12lb mirror carp. There had been so little fuss, and no real drama, but the fish provided the perfect end to a memorable winter and made me realise that a change of plan can always save the day.

Len Arbery with his 24lb common carp taken from Redmire in July 1988.

THE OLD DOG'S DAY
by Len Arbery

For the start of this story, the clock needs to be turned back to the close-season in 1988. It was then that I became heavily involved in negotiations that ended most favourably with the Carp Society gaining control of the premier carp fishery in England – Redmire Pool. That first summer of its control, the Carp Society charged its members £100 each per week for the privilege of fishing the pool. Only three anglers were allowed to fish at any one time. My son Tony and I were the first to join the queue and Tony's friend, Keith Griffin, pleaded to join us. At last, the confirmation of our booking dropped through the letter box and our allotted date was the third week of July.

On arrival, Tony and Keith tossed a coin for the first choice of pitches. This was only fair as I had been to Redmire many times previously, having been a member of Jack Hilton's Redmire Syndicate from 1973–76 inclusive. It was decided that I would take my pick from what was left. Keith won and picked the Stumps, as this had the reputation of being

the most consistent pitch on the pool at that time. Tony decided on the Evening pitch, so both of them were fishing on the east bank. I

Keith Griffin adjusting his tackle in the Stumps pitch, Redmire Pool, July 1988.

elected to start in the most historic place of all, the Willow pitch, for it was from this exact spot that Dick Walker captured that most momentous of carp, Clarissa, his 44lb record, more than three and a half decades earlier. This meant that I would be fishing the deep water close to the dam from the opposite, west, bank.

Keith and Tony are very modern carp anglers and are the owners of the latest tackle and experts in the most up-to-date methods and tactics. However, during the first forty-eight hours of the session, they reported no runs but constant half-hearted pulls which they put down to eels. Eel and gudgeon are the only species in Redmire apart from the carp.

The part of the pool where my baits lay seemed completely devoid of life and my buzzers were conspicuous by their total silence. Because of this and because to me, at least, it was not certain that the lads' abortive bites were from eels, I decided to move. Pitchford's Pit was my new choice, on the same bank as my companions and about midway between them. I pleaded age and they helped to move my gear into its position! I could see no future in fishing in a similar fashion to the boys so invested a couple of hours in thinking the problem through. The youngsters were using clipped-up bolt rig tactics and even their rods curved down tightly to the pull of their heavy leads. Perhaps that, I thought, was where the fault lay; perhaps there was simply too much resistance. Obviously if, as I belived, carp were responsible for those small indications, they wanted the bait and that was a good point. The bait at that moment was 16mm Richworth Birdfood Boilies. Gradually, it became clear to me what I should try, and once the plan was formulated I could hardly wait to begin.

My tackle was fished in what some might term old-fashioned, loose-line style. Even though my reels were Shimano Baitrunners, I would not even use that splendid facility in case it provided immeasurable resistance that the carp would not accept. Instead, my bail arms were left open. The rests were positioned low so that the rod tips, when lying in them, were

virtually submerged. The heavy, semi-fixed leads were exchanged for freely sliding $\frac{1}{4}$oz bombs on a 12in long link. Redmire Pool is a very ancient estate lake and consequently the bottom is covered in a layer of silt. The longish links, therefore, were to ensure the line rested on top of the silt rather than sinking down into it – another important thought in this quest for minimum resistance.

Using the above set-up did not provide immediate success. After casting out I had to wait *two hours* before the Optonic called out its strident warning. Going for the rod, I noticed the tiny piece of silver paper, previously held down with a coin to keep the line from spilling from the spool, hard against the butt-ring as the line poured out. After a very spirited struggle the first carp of the week was at last in my precious landing net. Not one to trouble the record fish committee I am sorry to say, but a 24lb Redmire common is still a very coveted prize.

During the remainder of our stay many more fine Redmire carp were caught, including several more twenties! My companions were quick to change to similar tactics, you see! Even they had to admit that on this occasion the Old Dog still had a trick or two up his sleeve.

The moral of this tale is plain for all to see: don't become blind or blinkered to change. From time to time even the very best of methods, bait and tactics may lose their effectiveness. Try not to follow others slavishly, especially if you have any information to go on, however insignificant it may at first appear. Always try to think how you can turn any pieces of knowledge to your advantage. I have lost count in my own career of how many times failure has been turned into success by a small but relevant change. Of course, as Dick Walker constantly reminded us, you won't get it right on every occasion, but often enough you will make the correct decision to make that change very worthwhile indeed.

KEEPING YOUR COOL
by Julian Cundiff

There is no doubt that you can make carp fishing as complicated or as basic as you want, despite what you read *ad nauseam* in the monthly papers. However, it is equally true to say that no matter how straightforward you try to keep your fishing, there are little edges and changes in approach that can pay real dividends. Indeed, many a time I have tried again and again with a trusted and proved tactic, only to find that a small alteration of details made all the difference indeed. One of these changes was keeping my baits frozen when fishing medium-length sessions with boilies.

I had been doing well at Tilery on my short sessions – just overnighters – but when I moved into fishing Friday mornings to Sunday nights things did not turn out quite as well as they should have done. The swim I had picked and kept baiting was indeed a productive one and one that, without a shadow of a doubt, the carp visited on each and every day. Situated on the tip of an island, the carp had to come across the baited area each evening as they travelled between the shallows and the deep water, so really, provided my rigs and presentation were sound, I should have caught each night. However, I only seemed to be succeeding the first night in and, no matter how many more nights I fished continuously, the second and third ones did not live up to the first. On seven occasions I had taken two or three carp on night one only to struggle to catch one more on the later two nights. What could be wrong?

At first I thought it could have been my continued presence in the swim for two or three days, but even when I bivvied up well back from the water and kept all movements to a minimum those runs still did not increase. The carp definitely still moved into the swim each evening (4.00pm to 2.00am) as liners, swirls and carp head and shouldering betrayed their presence conclusively. So why was I not getting those runs? Rigs, tactics, bait application were

Julian returns yet another super fish.

all closely examined, but I honestly could not see what the problem was.

Actually, it had been staring me in the face all the time – simply keeping my boilies frozen! When I was arriving Friday lunchtimes and baiting up, the hookbaits and freebies had been out of the freezer less than an hour and were frozen solid. Indeed, pushing a baiting needle through them proved to be difficult at times. At this stage in their life the baits were at their freshest and at their most attractive to the carp. However, by Saturday night when the baits had defrosted in the bag, the attraction level had dropped and, as I had experienced, the carp showed increasingly less interest. Simply, the bait was very effective on the first night but not so on subsequent nights. Quite why that should be I am still not sure, but other anglers who

149

have used high quality milk protein HNV baits know that what I am saying is right. Of course, the carp would still eat these baits, but they were not taking them with their initial gusto and were making fewer mistakes with the hook-baits as they examined them much more carefully.

Once I had found this answer to my problem it was simply a case of keeping my baits frozen all weekend in vacuum flasks and cool boxes and ensuring that Saturday's and Sunday's baits were frozen as solid as Friday's. Did all this work? Of course it did! From August onwards, once I had made the change, Saturday and Sunday nights proved to be just as productive as Fridays, excellent and conclusive proof that it is those small changes that can turn failure into success.

As a postscript perhaps you would be interested to know the recipe in question.

16oz of Nutrabaits Hi Nu Val
6 size 2 eggs
2mm SBS Cornish Ice Cream
1mm SBS Strawberry jam
6 drops Bergamot Essential Oil
1 level spoon Cotswold Baits Milk B plus
Colour - yellow
Boil for sixty seconds

THE IMPORTANCE OF USING YOUR EYES by John Watson

Early in the 1980s I decided to catch carp from a local gravel pit, my first experience of gravel pit carping. The water was, by reputation, very difficult and, after almost three months on the bank both day and night, I had caught no carp at all. Slowly, however, I began to know the water and, as I spent almost as much time with my line out of the water as in it, I felt success could not be far away. I had felt that a heavy baiting campaign would be the way to crack the nut, but after more fruitless weeks all I had to show for my efforts were tench, and lots of them. By this time I had tried everything from

my carp fishing repertoire: fishing on the bottom, on the surface, at night, in the middle of the day and through early morning pre-work sessions with still no success. Almost all baits had been used: paste, boilies, particles and an untold number of different floaters, but still the carp eluded me. I saw them almost everywhere, but I never found a spot where they fed or where they would beat the hordes of tench to the bait. Divine inspiration, I felt, was what I needed and without it I was surely doomed to failure. It was, however, not divine inspiration but luck which came to my rescue – or was it merely my love of blackberry pie?

One afternoon, after yet another blank session, I went to pick some blackberries before leaving for home. Stumbling down a very steep, overgrown bank I found myself staring at five large carp busily rooting about on a marginal gravel shelf. The shelf was only a couple of yards long, tucked in tight against the bank and masked from all sides by massive overhanging branches and trailing vegetation. Although the water was hardly a foot deep, the carp obviously felt secure and occasionally a wide back emerged from the water. I retreated very slowly, desperate not to spook the fish, and as I drove home I formulated a plan which I felt would at last produce a carp I had spent so long in pursuing.

As it was not possible to fish from the bank adjacent to the shelf because of the mass of foliage, I had no choice but to settle down on the bank opposite. There was a problem to all this: the tiny shelf was hedged in by brambles and there was a large willow tree growing at an angle of forty-five degrees over the exact spot where I wanted to put the baits. As a result, there was really no way I could cast a bait precisely. The solution was simple and on my return I set up with a 2oz bomb and a pike float which I cast across the lake, high into the branches of the willow tree. I then laid the rod down on the rests, walked around the lake and climbed the tree to retrieve the tackle. This done I replaced the bomb and float with fixed lead and baited hook, dropped it on to the shelf

John proudly shows off his well deserved prize.

along with a handful of freebies and returned to my swim. Darkness slowly descended and not a breath of air moved: I could hear the silence.

The silence was shattered by the scream of the Optonic as an unseen fish bolted to my right. The hook was well set and after a few tense moments I slipped the net under a fish that had eluded me through one of the most frustrating summers of my life. The torch revealed a superb mirror which in the light of dawn registered 23lb 4oz, my one and only from the pit as I did not return, feeling satisfied with a real reward for opportunism.

LIVENING UP THE FLOATER
by Chris Currie

Perhaps the best example I can give of how a very small change indeed can lead to success in carp fishing concerns the relationship between the hook and the floating bait. I have lost count of the times that I have watched carp approach a small floating bait only for them to turn away at the last moment, spooked by the way the floater sits in the water quite differently to the free offerings they have been feeding on previously.

Any floating bait is affected by the presence of a hook in it. Take Chum Mixers as an example. Most of the baits in an average box of Chum will not be large enough to counteract the weight of the hook, so they have a tendency to tip slightly in the water. The result is that they do not behave naturally and on most waters that will mean rejection by fish.

The solution is straightforward. Before beginning to fish, the largest twenty or thirty Mixers from the batch are taken out and kept separately as hookbaits. Nicking the hook in one end and allowing the shank to stand free of the bait will cause a hook to throw the bait out of balance again and so this too fails to achieve the desired effect. The bait needs to be hooked in such a way that the shank lies the full length of the bait. This simple attention to detail, plus the added buoyancy of the slightly larger bait, virtually eliminates fish spooking on all but the most overfished of waters.

Fishing floaters in winter is not generally considered to be worth while, which is good news for me as it leaves a whole avenue of fish catching unexploited. The fish may be wary in the extreme of summer floaters, but, if they have never been used in winter, it is almost as though they have never seen the approach before. However, do not expect carp to rush around after baits like they do in the summer, as this happens very rarely indeed.

Winter fish need a new approach. It is no good throwing baits out to drift around until the fish find them, because that just will not work. You need to have a good idea of where the fish are lying up, often in a state of semi-hibernation. Snaggy areas are best, particularly old reed-beds. These may be extremely difficult to fish in summer, but they are seldom very threatening in winter. You might not be able to see the fish, but on nine lakes out of ten these are favoured winter 'sleeping quarters'.

To catch the fish you need to put the floaters out well in advance. This is why so few people believe in winter floaters, because they wait an hour or two and, when nothing happens, they give up. You must remember that nothing will happen for at least two hours on most waters. You often need to rebait the area to replenish depredations made by ducks, but it is often three or four hours after first putting the bait out that the fish start to take them. You will need to be very sharp to spot them and move

Chris Currie displays the fruits of winter floater fishing.

very slowly, sipping in the baits with the most minimum of disturbances. The slightest noise will put them down in the first few minutes of feeding and, once they start taking well, you should allow them to build up their confidence before putting your bait to one of the larger fish.

Winter fish often move slowly and deliberately, so it is absolutely essential to use a carefully balanced hookbait. It was fishing for carp in the winter that made me realize the necessity of having the bait correctly balanced. Provided the fish are known to take floaters in the summer, I have yet to find a water where the method has not worked once the fish are lying up. If you give it a proper try, exactly as I have described, you will probably surprise yourself.

THE SINGLE AAA SHOT
by Tony Miles

Even after thirty years of specimen hunting, I am still amazed at how often the most insignificant detail can separate success from failure. With no species is this more true than with carp, whose size, power and cunning soon expose any deficiency in technique.

Several years ago, when I first began to use the bolt rig that is still my main choice for carp, I endured a day of total frustration before I finally sorted out what was wrong. The rig in question was a standard arrangement of an in-line drilled lead, with a braided hook length and a length of rig tubing the other, the hook length being shorter than the tubing thereby making the rig virtually tangle free. Hook-link swivel and tubing are connected to the bore tube of the bomb by short lengths of slightly wider gauge rig tubing, so making the rig semi-fixed.

The carp were very active on my first day with this rig and milled around over my bed of peanut-flavoured boilies from first light. So frequent were the rolls and swirls that the fish had to be feeding hard and yet by dusk the only action I had experienced was a fish, that I pulled out after a few seconds.

As the light began to fade there were four screaming runs in quick succession, each of which was missed completely without giving the slightest resistance. I started to mess around with hook-link lengths, but that was not the answer either. Two more runs were missed in the night and then, at dawn, I hooked a good fish which I saw boil at the surface before it, too, came adrift. On retrieving my terminal rig, I noticed a big mirror scale on the hook-point. Immediately, with proof of foul hooking, I realized that the missed bites could probably have been liners caused by carp bolting, but what was causing this behaviour?

Tony Miles with another beauty.

As soon as I examined the rig in the marginal shallows, the answer came to me. There, standing proudly to attention, at an angle of forty-five degrees was the 18in (46cm) rig tubing. If anything was designed to frighten fish and promote false bites, that was! I soon realized that, despite the fine bore of the tube, it still contained entrapped air which was causing the buoyancy I was witnessing. The problem was solved simply by pinching on an AAA on the line at the top of the tubing, whereupon it lay obediently flat and unobtrusive on the lake bed.

That ridiculously simple adjustment to my presentation made the vital difference. On the second day, I went on to enjoy a further five runs, each of which resulted in a solidly hooked and landed carp to just under 20lb. It seemed incredible that a single AAA shot could make all the difference between success and failure in carp fishing – but that was the case that particular day.

8 LEST WE FORGET

In the end, it has to be said that fishing in our society is for fun and not food, sport and not survival, and that carp are only fish. That word 'only', though, has wide and often painful connotations. I remember an article many years ago in, I believe, *Carp* magazine when the author, Bill Philips, lost two large fish in a single session on that notoriously difficult water, the School Pool. He said that at the time and for a few weeks following, not only his fishing but his work and social life were severely affected. Bill continued by saying that he appreciated that his reactions to these lost fish had been extreme and he pleaded to his readers to 'Fish for pleasure, not obsession: it could save you a breakdown!'

Following this same tack, I will quote from Kevin Clifford, whom I contacted for help with this book, but, happy man that he is, he was able to reply in this way:

I am afraid I cannot, in all honesty, tell you about any carp capture that posed some unusual or difficult problem. In reality, none of my big carp were difficult to catch; in fact, in general, the majority of big carp are particularly easy to catch – the characteristics of king carp make them inherently greedy – compared to some other species of coarse fish.

I could spice up a tale or two, but that would be dishonest. Almost all of my fish have been very easily caught. I have never wanted to chase a handful of big fish in some huge water, as I enjoy a bend in my rod too much! On the odd time that I have gotten into that area, I have soon become cheesed off!

Kevin Clifford is one of the sanest, most intelligent men in fishing today and he is quite right to stress the important point about enjoyment. I think we can all accept that. However, is he more than half right when we look at the ease or difficulty of capturing the carp? Certainly, the very volume of food a king carp needs to consume renders it susceptible to a mistake sooner or later. Yet, very often, as we all know, this mistake comes later.

I remember the great debate back in the 1960s over carp and intelligence and Richard Walker's assertion that they were guided by conditioned reflex rather than objective reasoning ability. Pavlov's dogs were frequently brought into the subject, creatures that salivated at the sound of bells that heralded food. Carp, Walker said, showed similar responses and, of course, they still do. But then, so do humans if you have seen them in a pub when last orders are called. None of this proves to me that humans or dogs are guided by conditioned reflex alone. The question is whether carp can assimilate facts and deduce anything from them rather than simply follow their instincts in a slavish fashion.

Des Woodhouse had a very large garden pond of perhaps half the size of a swimming pool. In it were a great number of koi carp of magnificent sizes and colours. I remember one hot afternoon many years ago when I went round to visit and he showed the fish off proudly. His small daughter began to feed the fish with bread from her fingers and from her toes. The carp sucked the food in greedily and noisily and without any apparent fear. Their reaction was the same when Des fed them, but when I tried the carp would not come within a yard of me. This could not have been con-

*One of the most beautiful carp I personally have seen a photograph of, even if it is slightly blurred!
John Nunn holds an absolutely awe-inspiring mid-twenty taken from a Suffolk water.*

ditioned reflex, for neither I nor anybody else had ever maltreated the carp in that pond. Surely they could differentiate between me and Des through either sight or smell and were suspicious of the difference. That cannot be conditioned reflex but rather suggests some type of reasoning power. Even survival instinct is not strong enough in this case, for the carp had been cosseted since the day they were spawned.

This is the sort of tale that could be repeated over and over again by most anglers of experience and many of us would have to conclude that the fish of most species show something resembling intelligence as we know it, even if on a low scale. The chess game that I talked

about at the beginning of this book becomes relevant to at least some degree.

If we accept that we are dealing with sentient beings, surely that puts even more onus on us to fish responsibly. There is, thankfully, a very strong move these days against leaving rods unattended. Similarly, those large multiple-bag shots of big fish are generally ignored. Can anyone really support two or three large fish without any risk of harm being done? Certainly, also, more anglers are aware of the need to look after valuable, even venerable, fish. It is a credit to us all that carp can be caught repeatedly without sustaining any obvious damage.

Here, though, is the rub. If we accept that our carp do show intelligence, no matter on what level, can there be any doubt that capture equals trauma? We do not want to be too precious here: provided that we treat them with respect, we probably do more good than harm by cherishing and protecting the waters that they inhabit – as long as, surely, we move on. When *we* have caught the carp of our dreams, when *our* challenge is satisfied, we must move on so that *others* can take up the running. To keep trying to catch the same fish repeatedly must be morally questionable. Take sparingly from this sport of ours and let us try to keep greed out of it.

Sadly, the gap between game and coarse fishermen continues to be wide and there is a debate in the trout and salmon magazines, over the question of whether game-fish should be killed or released. Hugh Falkus, who brought this debate into focus, makes the point that once we start releasing game-fish we are making toys of them and simply putting them through stresses for sport rather than for our stomachs. This is an interesting point and Mr Falkus says that by returning fish we are losing our credibility as hunters. Of course, even in

the game world, there have been many quick to reply, but it has to be said that the vast majority have come out in favour of the argument. If the game world is committed to killing and eating fish, it makes our own stance of catching carp repeatedly over the years an ever more dubious one. We have, I believe, to think very carefully about our position and everything we do. This does not mean that we have to be negative and defensive but we have to consider everything from every angle.

This, I know, has been a rambling sort of conclusion, raising all sorts of questions that have mostly gone unanswered. This, surely, is the nature of debate and hopefully, this book has been about debate virtually throughout. I hope that more carp will be caught by more anglers as a result of this book, but above all what I do hope is that readers will think even more deeply about what they do by the side of lake, pond, pit or river. This is the most satisfying sport, I believe, known to man, and if we give it less than our entire attention we do it less than justice.

BIBLIOGRAPHY

B.B., *The Fisherman's Bedside Book*, 1945

Bailey, John, *In Visible Waters*, Crowood Press, 1984

   – *In Wild Waters*, Crowood Press, 1989

Bailey, John, and Page, Martyn, *Carp – The Quest for the Queen*, Crowood Press, 1986

Ball, Chris, *The King Carp Waters*, Crowood Press, 1993

Boote, Paul and Wade, Jeremy, *Somewhere Down the Crazy River*, Sangha Books, 1992

Braddock, Archie, *Fantastic Feeder Fishing*, Pisces Angling Publications, 1992

Chapman, Matthew, *A Never Forgotten Dawn*, Oxford Brookes University, 1993

Clarke, Brian, *In Pursuit of Stillwater Trout*, A & C Black, 1975

Clifford, Kevin, *History of Carp Angling*

Guttfield, Frank, *In Search of Big Fish*, *Angling Times* Books, 1964

Hilton, Jack, *Quest for Carp*, Pelham Books, 1972

Venables, Bernard, *The Angler's Companion*, Allen & Unwin, 1959

Walker, Richard, *Drop Me a Line*, MacGibbon & Kee, 1953

   – *Stillwater Angling*, MacGibbon & Kee, 1953

   – *Walker's Pitch*

INDEX

Page references in italics denote illustrations.